# WORLD WAR I
# WITNESS ACCOUNTS

# WORLD WAR I
# WITNESS ACCOUNTS

EDITED AND COMPILED
BY JANICE ANDERSON

LORENZ BOOKS

This edition is published by Lorenz Books, an imprint of Anness Publishing Ltd,
108 Great Russell Street, London WC1B 3NA; info@anness.com

www.lorenzbooks.com; www.annesspublishing.com; twitter: @Anness_Books

Anness Publishing has a new picture agency outlet for images for publishing, promotions or advertising.
Please visit our website www.practicalpictures.com for more information.

A CIP catalogue record for this book is available from the British Library.

Produced by Omnipress Limited, UK
Cover design by Omnipress Limited, UK

JANICE ANDERSON was born and educated in New Zealand, but has lived for many years in Britain. After
working for some years as a newspaper journalist, charity press officer and editor for several of Britain's leading
illustrated non-fiction publishing companies, she became a freelance writer and editor, specialising in illustrated
non-fiction books. Like her late husband, Edmund Swinglehurst, with whom she has written several books, Janice
Anderson has written many non-fiction books, specialising in art, cinema, travel and social history.

# Contents

# Introduction

The outbreak of war in Europe in August 1914 marked the breakdown of a near-century-long series of alliances, treaties, ententes and 'understandings'. These had kept the continent as a whole at peace since 1815, when the Battle of Waterloo had finally destroyed the empire of Napoleon Bonaparte. During the century, Great Britain had grown into a rich imperial power, ruled by a sovereign, Victoria, Queen and Empress, whose children and grandchildren had married into many of the royal courts of Europe. She is said to have died, in 1901, in the arms of her grandson, Kaiser Wilhelm II of Germany.

The Kaiser may have loved his grandmother, but he certainly did not love Britain. His own imperial ambitions ensured that Germany would be the greatest threat to British power by the end of the nineteenth century, with a navy that could take on the power of the Royal Navy and an army that military strategists had ensured would be able to mobilise quickly and in strength at any threat. Away to the east, Russia, too, was flexing its imperial muscle. Then there was France, no longer an empire, but still with colonies in many parts of the world, and the lumbering Austro-Hungarian Empire. In the first decade of the twentieth century, these powers had a worldwide network of colonies and trading connections, which new communications technologies ensured were closely linked to them.

When the heir to the throne of Austria and Hungary, the Archduke Franz Ferdinand, and his wife were assassinated in the Bosnian capital, Sarajevo, on 28 June 1914, the chancelleries and foreign offices of Europe – and the newspapers of Europe – were rapidly informed of the crime. Within a month, those shots from the revolver of a 19-year-old Serbian student called Gavrilo Princip had brought down the carefully balanced framework of treaties and alliances in Europe. Russia, knowing how long it took to get its forces together, issued mobilisation orders. Austria, receiving little satisfaction from Serbia in the matter of pursuing assassins, on 28 July officially declared war on Serbia, which was already partially mobilised. Russia came in on the side of Serbia, prompting Germany to issue ultimata to Russia, and, to ensure that it would not be attacked on two fronts at once, to France. By 3 August these ultimata had become declarations of war.

It was Germany's advance on France, involving the crossing of the Belgian frontier and therefore ignoring Belgian neutrality, that brought Great Britain into the war. Britain was, in fact, something of an unknown quantity as far as war in Europe went. Its position as the world's greatest power at the time, coupled with its extremely strong navy, ensured that any war involving Britain would take on a world dimension, and that Britain would be a major player in any great conflict in Europe. But its army was not considered of much account – a 'contemptibly small army' the Kaiser called it. His remark, translated into English, became 'a small, contemptible army', leading to the nickname 'Old Contemptibles' for the soldiers of the British Expeditionary Force that went to France in 1914.

German military strategists, when planning their tactics for the major war that they were sure would come in Europe early in the twentieth century, had not expected to be halted on their planned march to Paris. When they were, because Britain and France put up enough troops and armaments to confront and halt them, both sides became bogged down in a war of attrition. This was carried out from hundreds of miles of trenches, dugouts and shell holes, stretching from Switzerland to the Channel coast, with advances and retreats being measured in yards, rather than miles.

The first world war of the twentieth century was a war marked by greater devastation and larger numbers of casualties, of both fighting men and civilians, than had ever been seen before. On the first day of the Battle of the Somme 60,000 men were killed or wounded; it was the largest military disaster in history.

Far-reaching heavy artillery, the tank, fighter and bomber aeroplanes, and gas – all the great death-dealing agents of twentieth-century war – were introduced to an increasingly appalled world during World War I. And it was during this war that mass genocide first became a weapon of warfare, when the Ottoman Empire forcibly drove between two and three million Armenians out of eastern Anatolia in 1915. About a third of them were massacred, and another third perished on their way out of Anatolia.

A handful of European countries – Spain, Switzerland, the Netherlands, and the Scandinavian nations – managed to remain neutral throughout the war. But Bulgaria, Romania and Greece were all sucked into the conflict – as was China which, attacked by Japan, entered the war on the side of the Allies in 1917. Most of the countries of the British Empire, including Australia, Canada, India, New Zealand and South Africa, sent troops and nursing detachments to the aid of the Allies, as did many of France's colonies.

Most decisive of all, when both sides in the conflict in Europe were nearing exhaustion both morally and in terms of the number of troops they could get to the Front, the United States entered the war on the side of the Allies in 1917, eventually sending some two million troops to Europe. Germany, fearing the arrival of American troops and able to release thousands of troops from the Russian front after Russia, plunged into the chaos of revolution, withdrew, put everything they had into a major push in the spring of 1918. The Allies reeled, fell back, and then stood firm. After a summer and autumn of intense fighting, Germany surrendered, with most of its troops still in France and Belgium.

The war which ended on the eleventh hour of the eleventh day of the eleventh month of 1918 had lasted for 1,551 days and had claimed the lives of nine million fighting men, and thousands more men and women behind the battle lines and at home. The politicians had called it the war to end all wars. It did not do so. Indeed, the peace settlement, ending in the Treaty of Versailles in 1919, left so many problems unsettled, so many questions unanswered that within two decades Europe was at war again.

# WAR IS DECLARED

# War is Declared

When Europe went to war on 4 August 1914, it was generally believed in Britain that it would all be over in about four months, and all the men would be home in time for Christmas, if not for the start of the new term at Oxford. In France, enthusiasm for the war was intensified by the belief that France could now get back its Alsace-Lorraine lands lost to Germany after the 1870 war. 'To Berlin!' was the cry that went up in Paris.

In both Britain and France the declaration of war led very quickly to the expression of anti-German feelings so strong that there were riots and lootings of shops owned by Germans or people who were thought to be German. The British government's anti-German policy during World War I, which included internment for years for many thousands of German men, caused more than a little shame after the war ended.

The British military authorities, led by the iconic figure of Field Marshal Earl Kitchener, Secretary of State for War, aimed to send an army a million strong to Europe. Clearly, there would have to be a massive recruitment campaign to get volunteers, as the regular Army, which went to France as the British Expeditionary Force, and the Territorials could not on their own provide anything like this number.

Soon, a poster showing Lord Kitchener apparently pointing straight at every man in the country and telling him to join his country's army was appearing on every wall, fence and advertising hoarding in the country, and in every newspaper and magazine. Many employers, fired with patriotic fervour, also began to push their workers into joining up. The *Daily Sketch* newspaper, for instance, told its readers on 29 August that it was prepared to give any of its employees who volunteered a minimum of four weeks' full pay, after which married men would receive half-pay for the whole time they were on military duty. All men would, of course, be re-engaged when the war was over.

Spurred on by the suggestion in the *Daily Sketch*, the Council of the Football Association began looking at forming Footballers' Battalions from the 7,000 players in England's professional football teams. Eventually, five Sportsmen's battalions were raised in Britain. The 1st (Footballers)

Battalion included Walter Tull, a black player with Tottenham Hotspur, who became the first black officer in the British Army.

Kitchener's New Army included 144 battalions raised and paid for (except for their weapons which were the Army's responsibility) by local authorities and private bodies. Many men volunteered together, encouraged by the enthusiastic suggestion of politicians that they could all be 'pals' or 'chums' together while serving together. One consequence of this raising of whole battalions of 'pals' from one town, village or local area meant that as the war settled into the appalling attrition of trench warfare and more and more of those 'pals' were slaughtered, so the towns and villages they came from lost an entire generation of young men.

But even Lord Kitchener's charisma could not win enough volunteers to replace the thousands of casualties of the first months of the war, especially as it could take anything up to a year to get such raw recruits trained to a level where they could be of use in the trenches of the Western Front. In October, 1915, the Earl of Derby, Director of Recruitment, devised a new recruitment scheme that asked all men of military age, that is, from age 18 to 40, to register voluntarily – or 'attest' – for military service. They would be called up in batches by age, and with single men being considered before married men. Originally, the scheme was to be open until 15 December 1915, but so great was the last-minute rush to be attested that recruiting offices ran out of forms and there were not enough doctors to carry out all the necessary medical inspections. The deadline had to be extended.

Among the unforeseen consequences of this mass call-up into the armed forces of the nation's younger men was that it deprived factories and manufacturers, including those producing armaments, of far too many of their skilled workers. By May 1915, the British army was so short of high-explosive artillery shells that it had to ration them, notably during the offensive at Aubers Ridge and Festubert, which stalled as a result.

The jingoistic fervour that gripped the nation in August 1914 inspired thousands of teenage boys to lie about their age and join up. The Army did take boys as young as 17, but not until they were 19 could they be allowed to serve with the Expeditionary Force overseas. That was the theory, anyway, but when a fit and active boy stood in front of recruiting officers and said that he was 20, and followed this up by lying on his attestation forms, few of those officers were going to delve deeply into his age.

August 1914's jingoism aroused in many people, young women especially, an openly-expressed contempt for men who remained at home out of uniform. The Order of the White Feather, founded by a former admiral, Charles Fitzgerald, in 1914, soon recruited many women to its cause. Letters criticising 'flannelled fools' still playing cricket, or selfish footballers still turning out for their clubs, began to appear in newspapers. Many young women took to carrying white feathers, which they gave to any man not in uniform they encountered. Other young women chose to make a more positive contribution to the war effort, joining such organisations as the new Voluntary Aid Detachments (VAD) and the Women's Emergency Corps.

## The Archduke Franz Ferdinand of Austria

*The shooting in Sarajevo on 28 June 1914 sparked war throughout Europe.*

The Archduke Franz Ferdinand of Austria, nephew of the aged emperor and heir to the throne, was assassinated in the streets of Sarajevo, the Bosnian capital, yesterday afternoon. His wife, the Duchess of Hohenberg, was killed by the same assassin. Some reports say that the duchess was deliberately shielding her husband from the second shot when she was killed. One victim was struck in the body and the other in the face; the telegrams are contradictory about which wound the archduke suffered and which his wife.

The Manchester Guardian, *29 June 1914.*

> One victim was struck in the body and the other in the face . . .

## Hilaire Belloc in 'The Cruise of the Nona'

*Describes his glimpse of the mobilisation of the British Grand Fleet in 1914.*

When I set out from Plymouth there was nothing but rumour, nothing certain. The Fleet had already dispersed some days past from the great review at Spithead, and was, as we were told, in the Atlantic at manoeuvres…

Nothing was further from my mind than war and armament as the sun rose on that glorious July morning, right out of a clean horizon, towards which the wind blew fresh and cool… In this loneliness and content, as I sailed northward, I chanced to look out after an hour's steering or so, eastward again towards the open sea – and then it was that there passed me the vision I shall remember for ever, or for so long as the longest life may last.

Like ghosts, like things themselves made of mist, there passed between me and the newly risen sun, a procession of great forms, all in line, hastening eastward. It was the Fleet recalled.

The slight haze along that distant water had thickened, perhaps, imperceptibly; or perhaps the great speed of the men-of-war buried them too quickly in the distance. But, for whatever cause, this marvel was of short duration.

Then I knew that war would come.

> Like ghosts …
> between me and the
> newly risen sun …

*From* The Cruise of the Nona*, Hilaire Belloc, Constable & Co., 1928.*

## Sir Edward Grey, Britain's Foreign Secretary from 1905 to 1916

*Tells how he came to make a famous remark about the Great War.*

My recollection of those three days, August 1, 2 and 3 is one of almost continuous cabinets and of immense strain; but of what passed in discussion very little remains in my mind... There was little for me to do; circumstances and events were compelling decision...

A friend came to see me on one of the evenings of last week – he thinks it was on Monday, August 3rd. We were standing at a window of my room in the Foreign Office. It was getting dusk, and the lamps were being lit in the space below... My friend recalls that I remarked on this with the words 'The lamps are going out all over Europe: we shall not see them lit again in our lifetimes.'

> The lamps are going out all over Europe: we shall not see them lit again in our lifetimes.

*From* Twenty-five Years, 1892-1916, *Viscount Grey of Fallodon, London, 1925*

## King George V

*The king's entry in his diary for the day war was declared.*

August 4th. Warm, showers and windy.
At work all day. Winston Churchill came to
report at 1.0 that at the meeting of the
Cabinet this morning we had sent an
ultimatum to Germany that if by midnight
tonight she did not give satisfactory answer
about her troops passing through Belgium,
Goschen would ask for his passports. Held a
Council at 4.00. … I held a Council at 10.45
to declare War with Germany, it is a terrible
catastrophe but it is not our fault… When
they heard that War had been declared the
excitement (of the crowds outside the
Palace) increased & it was a never to be
forgotten sight when May and I with David
[the Prince of Wales, later Edward VIII]
went on to the balcony, the cheering was
terrific. Please God it may soon be over &
that he will protect dear Bertie's life…

Please God it may soon be over & that he will protect dear Bertie's life …

## W. McQueen Pope, social historian

*Recalls the atmosphere in London on 3–4 August 1914.*

The British Government sent an ultimatum to the German Government that unless they cleared out [of Belgium] by midnight on 4th August 1914, a state of war would exist between the two countries...

Outside Buckingham Palace stood a massed throng, cheering and singing. At Westminster, taut-faced statesmen waited the answer which never came. The Middle Classes all over the country and in that crowd were entering their final phase and did not know it. Never again would gold coins in their pockets be paid into their banks, be their safeguard in life. Never again would they need those sovereign purses so many of them carried that day. Strangers spoke to each other. Men met other men they had not seen for years. 'What are you going to do?' asked one young man of an old schoolfellow met in that crowd by chance. 'I've put my name down for the Westminster Dragoons,' said the other. 'I'm trying to get there now, but I'm stuck in this mob. How about you?' 'I don't know yet,' said the other. 'The Navy, if they'll have me.' They shook hands and wished each other luck. The crowd pushed them apart. They never met again. There were many little things like that in London on that night when the world changed and the golden sovereign died.

*From* Twenty Shillings in the Pound, *Hutchinson & Co., 1948.*

## Ambroise Vollard, art dealer

*Recalls the atmosphere in Paris after the ordering of a*
*general mobilisation in France, 4 August, 1914.*

When Paris was threatened and began to empty of its inhabitants, I felt some anxiety about a friend of mine who must, I thought, be in difficulties, with a wife and eleven children. He was too old to be called up, and as they had a house in the country I should not have been surprised to find their Paris one empty. But my friend was there in his shirt sleeves, sawing wood in the little garden behind the house.

'You see,' he said to me, 'I'm developing my muscles, so as to be able to join up.'

On leaving this hero I met a little boy crying on the pavement. I asked the reason for his tears.

> Grandpa said the man must be a Boche . . .

'When our grocer was supposed to have gone off to the War,' the brat explained, 'Grandpa said the man must be a Boche, and we'd go with a few good Frenchmen and revictual ourselves from his shop, and we'd eat little fishes in tins and green peas in bottles; but the grocer's wife smelt a rat and sent for the police.'

*From* Recollections of a Picture Dealer, *Ambroise Vollard; English translation, Little, Brown and Co., Boston, 1936.*

## Claude Monet, artist

*Writes to the radical journalist Gustave Geffroy. Monet's house and garden at Giverny was close enough to the Western Front to be within sound of the gunfire.*

…One thing I know is that in the present state of things and in my isolation, a letter from a good friend like you is a comfort which makes these anxieties easier to bear. Most of my family has left me with no knowledge of their whereabouts; only my son Michel who has been temporarily discharged is with me, along with Blanche [Monet's stepdaughter]… a mad panic has swept our area…As for myself, I'm staying here regardless and if those savages insist on killing me, they'll have to do it in the midst of my paintings, before my life's work.

*Giverny, 1 September 1914.*

> As for myself, I'm staying here regardless and if those savages insist on killing me …

## Corporal Stefan Westmann, 29th Division, German army

*Recalls hearing about receiving his call-up papers while he was a medical student.*

I was a medical student when I received my call-up papers. They ordered me to report for military duty in a clean state and free of vermin at an infantry regiment in Freiburg, in Baden. We had no idea of any impending war... We served in our blue and red uniform, but on the 1st of August mobilisation orders came and we put on our field grey. At 2 o'clock in the morning of the 4th of August we marched out of Freiburg with torches – silent, without any music, and with no enthusiasm. We were really weighed down by our kit, which weighed 75lb [33.75kg] per man. We crossed the Rhine over a very wobbly pontoon bridge into Alsace.

... silent, without any music, and with no enthusiasm.

*Extract from a tape recording in the Imperial War Museum, published in* Forgotten Voices of the Great War, *Max Arthur, Ebury Press, in association with the Imperial War Museum, 2002.*

## Robert Graves, writer

*Aged nineteen when war was declared, Robert Graves served on the Western Front for much of the war.*

I had just finished with Charterhouse and gone up to Harlech, when England declared war on Germany. A day or two later I decided to enlist. In the first place, though the papers predicted only a very short war – over by Christmas at the outside – I hoped that it might last long enough to delay my going to Oxford in October, which I dreaded. Nor did I work out the possibilities of getting actively engaged in the fighting, expecting garrison service at home, while the regular forces were away. In the second place, I was outraged to read of the Germans' cynical violation of Belgian neutrality.

> ...the papers predicted only a very short war – over by Christmas at the outside ...

*From* Goodbye To All That, *Robert Graves; Jonathan Cape, 1929, rev. ed. 1957.*

## Frank Lindley

*A fourteen-year-old boy who said he was twenty when he joined up in 1914.*

Me and my dad were getting ready to go to work and a knock came at the door and there was a telegram sudden just like, about 9a.m., and it said sorry to tell you that your Harry's at bottom. [drowned when the cruiser HMS *Hawke* was torpedoed in the North Sea in October 1914.] We read the bugger and we both collapsed. That finished my dad…[and] it upset the family a great deal. It made me think a bit. Everybody was wanting us, Kitchener was pointing, so I joined up. I wanted to avenge Harry's death. That was the main issue.

> …there was a telegram … it said sorry to tell you that your Harry's at bottom.

*Quoted in* Boy Soldiers of the Great War, *Richard van Emden, Headline Book Publishing, 2006.*

## Horace Calvert

*A fourteen-year-old lad from Bradford.*

I was going home from work… and as I got up the top of Richmond Road by the University of Bradford, there was a newsagent's shops and outside there was a big placard: 'War declared on Germany'. Mobilization had take place. I went to Bellevue Barracks, home of the 6th West Yorks, a Territorial battalion, and found there were crowds round there. Everybody was excited and every time they saw a soldier he was cheered. It was very patriotic and people were singing 'Rule Britannia', 'Land of Hope and Glory', all the favourites… quite a number were already setting off to enlist.

> … people were singing 'Rule Britannia', 'Land of Hope and Glory', all the favourites …

*Quoted in* Boy Soldiers of the Great War, *Richard van Emden, Headline Book Publishing, 2006.*

## Norman Demuth

*A rifleman with the London Rifle Brigade describes life before joining the army.*

As well as being given white feathers, there was another method of approach. You would see a girl come towards you with a delightful smile all over her face and you would think to yourself, 'My word this is somebody who knows me'. When she got to about five or six paces from you she would suddenly freeze up and walk past you with a look of utter contempt and scorn as if she could have spat. That was far more hurtful than a white feather... I was given a white feather when I was sixteen, just after I had left school. I was looking in a shop window and I felt somebody press something into my hand and I found it was a woman giving me a white feather.

# . . . a look of utter contempt and scorn as if she could have spat.

*From* Forgotten Voices of the Great War, *Max Arthur, Ebury Press, in association with the Imperial War Museum, 2002.*

## Alexander Powell, American newspaper correspondent

*Reporting the German advance on France through Belgium for the New York newspaper* The World *in August 1914.*

It was a sight never to be forgotten. As far as the eye could see stretched solid columns of marching men, pressing westward, ever westward. The army was marching in three mighty columns along three parallel roads. These dense masses of moving men in their elusive blue-grey uniforms looked for all the world like three monstrous serpents crawling across the countryside...

We passed regiment after regiment, brigade after brigade, of infantry, and after them hussars, Uhlans, cuirassiers, field batteries, more infantry, more field guns, ambulances, then siege guns, each drawn by thirty horses, engineers, telephone corps, pontoon wagons, armoured motor cars, more Uhlans, the sunlight gleaming on their forest of lances, more infantry in spiked helmets, all sweeping by as irresistible as a mighty river, with their faces turned towards France.

> The army was marching in three mighty columns ...

*Quoted in* Pals on the Somme 1916, *Roni Wilkinson, Pen & Sword Military, 2006.*

## Sydney Bond

*A Liverpool schoolboy recalls how his playground was commandeered to provide a training ground for some of the huge numbers of volunteers in 1914.*

Opposite to where we lived was the Wavertree Playground, a huge place bequeathed to the children of the district and marvellous for football, and then it was suddenly taken from us. I only had to go into this playground to see men practising throwing a bomb. They made a few slit trenches and put blokes in there and the sergeant would try to teach them to lob a bomb over, and that went on continually.

> I only had to go into this playground to see men practising throwing a bomb.

*From* All Quiet on the Home Front, *Richard van Emden and Steve Humphries, Headline Book Publishing, 2003.*

## Herbert Innel Minchin

*Served with the Machine Gun Corps, 54th Battalion, 34th Division in France and Belgium.*

On Dec. 10 1915, myself and Charles Hanger, who worked with me on the *Newark Herald* attested and became soldiers awaiting orders to 'fall in'. Being among the latter married groups, we had a fairly long spell before our services were required, but about the middle of June 1916, we received notice to report a fortnight later.

July 1 [we] left Newark in a carriage that was locked (the first stage of army discipline)… My first Army meal not very encouraging. This was tea, or what passed for the name of it. There were two huge pieces of bread and margarine and a basin of tea. My tea basin was decorated with pieces of carrot and other remains of dinner…

Next morning was a very full one. The most momentous was the meeting with 'Dr. Crippen', the nickname those already in barracks had bestowed on the Medical Officer. His rank and name was Major Bennett. 'Crippen' suited him much better. He was a brute and woe betide the man who tried to 'swing the lead'.

The newcomers were paraded before him and in less then ten minutes I was vaccinated and inoculated. Many men

*From document Minchin H. I., 06/55/1 in the Documents Department in the Imperial War Museum.*

The most momentous was the meeting with 'Dr. Crippen', the nickname those already in barracks had bestowed on the Medical Officer.

could not stand the double doses, and they were fainting in all directions. To one man he said, 'You should have been in France and buried a long time ago.' Another man who answered back when he was spoken to, was vaccinated eight times on one arm. To me he was kind enough to say that I should have been in the Guards and not in the Army Service Corps. For 48 hours after inoculation we were allowed the privilege of doing nothing, and in fact we were too ill to do anything.

## Corporal R. G. Plint

*Plint became a signaller in the 'Bankers' Battalion, 26th Royal Fusiliers, because at his interview he confessed to knowing semaphore.*

In the latter half of 1915 a circular went out to all banks and their branches calling for the formation of a 'Bankers' Battalion of the Royal Fusiliers, application to be made to a Colonel North down in the south, and a letter was sent out to all who were accepted, which had to be presented to the Recruiting Officer.

Towards the end of 1915 I presented my letter at the Recruiting Office, Whitechapel, Liverpool. Three of us from the Bank of Liverpool applied to join up, but I was the only one to pass the tests. A week later I reported to the London headquarters of the Battalion and was transported to High Beccles, Epping Forest, where I was kitted out apart from a greatcoat.

> . . . I was the
> only one to pass
> the tests.

*From document R. G. Plint MM, 80/19/1 in the Documents Department of the Imperial War Museum.*

## Kitty Eckersley

*A mill worker who didn't want to lose her husband and didn't want him to go at all.*

We had a friend in Canada who had enlisted over there and when he came back he … booked seats for the Palace and would we like to go? We didn't know what was on, of course, but it was a great treat for us. So we went. And when we got there everything was lovely. Vesta Tilley was on stage. She was beautifully dressed in a lovely gown of either gold or silver. But what we didn't know until we got there was that also on stage were Army officers with tables all set up for recruiting. She introduced those songs, 'We Don't Want to Lose You, But We Think You Ought To Go' and 'Rule Britannia'… Then she came off the stage and walked all round the audience – up and down, either side, down the middle – and the young men were getting up and following her… She put her hand on my husband's shoulder – he was on the end seat – and as the men were all following her, he got up and followed her too.

## … when we got there everything was lovely.

*From* Forgotten Voices of the Great War, *Max Arthur, Ebury Press, in association with the Imperial War Museum, 2002.*

## Reports in the *Barnsley Chronicle* newspaper
*Reporting on the days after the declaration of war.*

# ... they have been inundated with applications from willing recruits ...

Clerks have been busy for hours daily taking names, and late last night there was no falling off in numbers of Volunteers. The names of hundreds of men have been taken over and above the numbers required to complete the establishment of the 5th Battalion York and Lancaster Regiment, the 6th West Yorkshire Regiment, the Royal Horse Artillery – Wentworth, and the West Riding Field Ambulance Corps... Such a noble response has been made for volunteers to go to the seat of war that the supply of documents used for this purpose gave out on Wednesday. The recruiting officer and the magistrates of Barnsley have been inundated with applications from willing recruits...

*Quoted in* Pals on the Somme 1916, *Roni Wilkinson, Pen & Sword Military, 2006.*

## From the *Daily News* newspaper, 4 August 1914

In London, the people's enthusiasm culminated outside Buckingham Palace when it became known that war had been declared . . . The news was received with tremendous cheering, which grew to a deafening roar when King George, Queen Mary and the Prince of Wales appeared.

Westminster, Charing Cross and the main thoroughfares round Westminster were thronged all last night with excited crowds. Union Jacks were everywhere to be seen, and the air was filled with the sound of patriotic songs; Trafalgar Square was almost impassable. A hostile crowd assembled outside the German embassy and smashed the windows.

The news was received with tremendous cheering, which grew to a deafening roar . . .

## Elfie Druhm

*Recalls how her German father and English mother and their salon in London became the targets of mob anti-German feeling in 1914.*

The anti-German feeling from the first was terrific. The government and the press stirred up the hatred. Our shop was smashed within a couple of weeks of the war breaking out and we had to leave because there was so much hostility there... Father was taken away [to four years' internment], and Mother left at the same time. We had nowhere to go and we had to find furnished rooms very quickly... My mother tried to find work telling the truth, saying who she was, why she was looking for a job and where her husband was. Nobody would help because she was married to a German, even though she was totally English... So she changed her name to Miss Norris, her maiden name, and as soon as she went as Miss Norris she was employed at a salon in Oxford Street.

Nobody would help her because she was married to a German...

*Quoted in* All Quiet on the Home Front, *Richard van Emden and Steve Humphries, Headline Book Publishing, 2003.*

# VOICES FROM
# THE FRONT

# Voices from the Front

The first contingent of the British Army to arrive in France disembarked on 7 August 1914. These troops, part of the British Expeditionary Force, were all highly-trained regulars. Their Commander-in-Chief was General Sir John French who, when he arrived in France on 14 August, set up his headquarters in the Hotel du Rhin in Amiens. He was not there long. By 31 August Amiens had been captured by the Germans.

Within weeks the Allied armies had retreated from Mons and between 19 October and 22 November fought the first Battle of Ypres (or 'Wipers' as the British soldiers called it). By now, the casualties on both sides were enormous – some 58,000 killed, wounded and missing from the ranks of the BEF alone. The great Somme Offensive, which began on 1 July 1916, cost the British Army 420,000 men, with nearly 60,000 casualties on its first day – this despite a huge preliminary bombardment of the German lines day and night for five days.

Thus the Western Front became a place for death and destruction on a scale not seen before in the history of warfare. It was a place where millions of men lived like rats in deep, sand-bagged and barbed-wired trenches where the mud was often so thick they could be sucked to their deaths. They faced other men in other trenches separated by a No Man's Land that was a nightmare vision of water-logged shell holes, barbed wire, mud, bleak tree stumps and thousands of corpses and bits of bodies. In the trenches, lice and rats were constant companions, the rats growing to the size of cats as they fed on the corpses and body parts of the dead, and even on the food in the great coat pockets of sleeping soldiers. Trench foot was an ever-present problem and the sour taste of fear – fear of shelling and sniping, fear of mustard gas and chlorine gas (and increasingly diabolical mixtures of other gases devised by both sides as the war went on), and fear of being maimed – was in every mouth.

The British Army dealt with these fears by issuing rum regularly on the front line. The thick, dark and very strong rum came to the battlefield in large earthenware jars and flagons, shards of which still litter the battlefields, and was usually issued on a day-to-day basis and always before the men were due to go over the top. The effect of a tot of rum was wonderfully quick, able to warm a soldier from his frozen feet to his numb ears.

But rum could not deal with lice. One page in Corporal R. Chambers' diary/notebook, in the Imperial War Museum in London, is headed 'Specimen of the yellow-bellied louse'. Dominating the page are three small black splodges/smears, circled in pencil. Underneath them, Corporal Chambers, a stretcher-bearer in the 1st Battalion, Hertfordshire Regiment, wrote 'Caught and killed in the British trenches at Fonquevilliers – Feb 13th 1916, in the 19th month of this confounded War.'

In the early months of the war on the Western Front and, indeed, occasionally throughout it, fraternising with the enemy was not uncommon.

Sometimes, where No Man's Land was narrow enough, this could just be a bit of banter, such as 'Good morning, Fritz' shouted across No Man's Land. Sometimes gifts, such as packets of cigarettes, might be exchanged. The most famous example of fraternisation on the Western Front was the Christmas Truce of 1914. Soldiers often felt a stronger empathy with the enemy in their trenches on the other side of No Man's Land than with their own senior officers in their comfortable headquarters.

However, there was no fraternisation in the disastrous Gallipoli campaign, where Australians and New Zealanders, fighting for the Mother Country alongside British troops, endured appalling months boxed in between the sea and the cliffs of the Dardanelles coast. Other fronts were equally ferocious, with widespread death and destruction in Eastern Europe and on the borders with Russia (whose devastating losses in a disastrous war with Germany led to the Russian Revolution in 1917), in Italy, Greece, Egypt and Turkey.

## Colonel Charles Repington, military correspondent

*Reporting in* The Times, *Colonel Repington's despatch was the subject of heated discussion in the House of Commons just three days later.*

The results of our attacks on Sunday last in the districts of Frommelles and Richebourg were disappointing. We found the enemy much more strongly posted than we expected. We had not sufficient high explosive to level his parapets to the ground after the French practice... The want of an unlimited supply of high explosive was a fatal bar to our success. We have had many casualties this week, but if we have not won all we hoped, we have detained in our front a force equivalent to our own and greatly facilitated the French offensive on our right.

...But until we are thoroughly equipped for this trench warfare, we attack under grave disadvantages... If we can break through this hard outer crust of the German defences, we believe we can scatter the German armies, whose offensive causes us no concern at all.

But to break this hard crust we need more high explosive, more heavy howitzers, and more men. This special form of warfare has no precedent in history. It is certain we can smash the German crust if we have the means. So the means we must have, and as quickly as possible.

### ...we attack under grave disadvantages...

*Extracts from the famous 'Shell Despatch' in* The Times *newspaper, 14 May 1915.*

WORLD WAR I WITNESS ACCOUNTS

## H. S. Clapham

*Who served in the Honourable Artillery Company, recalling his first encounter with conscripts in 1915 in* Mud and Khaki: the Memories of an Incomplete Soldier, *Hutchinson, London, 1936.*

We were relieved by a North Country battalion of Kitchener's New Army – the first I have seen. They were rather quaint birds. They talked as if the War would be over in no time, now that they were out, but as soon as they got into the trench, a lot of them jumped on the fire-step, and started firing at our own line. We had to pull some of them down.

> Kitchener's New Army ... they were rather quaint birds.

*Quoted in* Call-To-Arms: The British Army 1914-18, *Charles Messenger, Cassell, 2006.*

## Albert 'Smiler' Marshall

*Who joined the Essex Yeomanry at seventeen and survived to be a centenarian.*

One day, the Germans sent a stick grenade flying over, to which they had tied a couple of cigarettes. After a bit, I went to the bomb, and my mates were saying, 'For God's sake don't touch it.' They thought the bomb would go off and blow me up. But I went and smoked a cigarette and it was all right, so we sent back the same stick bomb with a whole packet attached. I hope they enjoyed them.

'For God's sake don't touch it!' They thought the bomb would go off and blow me up.

*Quoted in* Boy Soldiers of the Great War, *Richard van Emden, Headline Book Publishing, 2006.*

## Note from the diary of Sister Jentie Paterson

*From Kelvinside, Glasgow, Sister Paterson was one of the first civilian nursing sisters to work near the front line in France.*

November 30 [1914] King expected [at St Omer]. Saw him pass through with Gen. French. Got a salute all to myself! His car carries the Royal Standard. French's the only car allowed to carry the Union Jack.

December 25, Friday. Xmas Day – well I hope I'll never have such another... Matron had me in her office & I arranged all Red X stores for her. Got packet of chocs. from Pr. Mary and Xmas Card from King and Queen. Daily Mail sent us Xmas puddings, otherwise we paid for our own turkeys etc.

Xmas Day – well
I hope I'll
never have such
another . . .

*Document file Paterson, J. Sister, 90/10/1 in the Documents Department of the Imperial War Museum.*

## David, Prince of Wales

*Nineteen-year-old David writes from the British Army Headquarters at St Omer, northern France, to a friend in March 1915.*

As you may imagine mine is a most rotten position in war time. I hold commissions in both services and yet I'm not allowed to fight. Of course I haven't got a proper job which is very painful to me and I feel I am left too much in a glass case.

I long to be taking my chance in the trenches with my brother officers and in fact all able-bodied Englishmen. But both seem to be impossible, so I have to carry on here at GHQ, attached to Divisions from time to time when all is quiet. . . This is a most rotten war unless you are actually fighting. It's a rotten war altogether and the sooner it ends the better for everyone concerned.

> This is a most rotten war unless you are actually fighting.

## Private Ernest Morley

*Describing Christmas 1914 on the Western Front to a fellow soldier in England.*

**Somewhere, France, 29/12/14**
We had decided to give the Germans a Christmas present of 3 carols & 5 rounds rapid. Accordingly as soon as night fell we started & the strains of 'While Shepherds' (beautifully rendered by the choir!) arose upon the air. We finished that and paused preparatory to giving the 2nd item on the programme. But lo! We heard answering strains arising from their lines. Also they started shouting across to us. Therefore we stopped any hostile operations and commenced to shout back. One of them shouted 'A Merry Christmas English. We're not shooting tonight.' We yelled back a similar message & from that time until we were relieved on Boxing morning @ 4 a.m. not a shot was fired.

After this shouting had gone on for some time they stuck up a light. Not to be outdone so did we. Then up went another. So we shoved up another. Soon the two lines looked like an illuminated fete. Opposite me they had one lamp and 9 candles in a row. And we had all the candles and lights we could muster stuck in our swords above the parapet. At 12.00 we sang 'God Save the King' &, with the exception of the sentries, turned in. Next morning, Christmas Day, they started getting out of the trenches & waving & some came over towards us. We went out and met them & had the curious pleasure of chatting with the men who had been doing their best to kill us, and we them.

I exchanged a cigarette for a cigar with one of them (not a bad exchange, eh?) & as some of them spoke English had quite a long conversation. One fellow said that as soon as the war was over he was 'going back to England by express'. He had a wife and 2 children in the Alexandra Rd!! They had no idea of where they were. Of course, they know the names of the towns through which they had passed but did not know what part of the map they were situated.

> One of them shouted 'A Merry Christmas English. We're not shooting tonight.'

*From document file E.G. Morley, 93/25/1 in the Documents Department of the Imperial War Museum.*

## Second Lieutenant Frank Potter

*Shortly after the first over-the-top attack of the Battle of the Somme began on 1 July 1916, Second Lieutenant Frank Potter was shot in the head and killed.*

**France 27/6/1916**

My dearest Mother and Father,

This is the most difficult letter I have ever sat down to write. We are going into an attack tomorrow and I shall leave this to be posted if I don't come back. It is a far bigger thing than I have ever been in before and my only hope is that we shall help in a victory that will bring the war nearer to a successful conclusion. I am hoping to have the nerve to keep my end up and to do my share – that is all that worries me at present. Of death I haven't any fear...

The worst of war is that one's people at home have to bear all the sacrifice and suffering. For my part I am content and happy to give my services and life to my country, but it is not my sacrifice, Mother and Dad, it is yours...

My fondest love to all at home
Your loving Son
Frank
XXXXXXX

*From* Pals on the Somme 1916 *by Roni Wilkinson, published 2006 by Pen and Sword Military, Barnsley, South Yorkshire.*

## British Officer Giles Eyre

*In* Somme Harvest, *his memoir of the Great War published in 1938.*

We are now scrambling over what must have been the British front-line trenches, a maze of humps and hillocks, half-filled-in ditches, mounds of faded and burst sandbags, barbed wire clumps sticking out here and there, shell-holes, smashed trench-boards and a litter of rusty tins, pieces of equipment, broken rifles and goodness knows what else. We strike out into what was once No Man's Land, a welter of confused destruction and shell-holes.

Here all the casualties have not been gathered in yet, and horrible looking bundles in Khaki, once men, still lie in shell-holes.

> ... mounds of faded and burst sandbags, barbed wire clumps sticking out here and there ...

*Quoted in* The Somme Then and Now, *John Giles; rev. ed. published by Battle of Britain Prints International Ltd, 1986.*

## C. E. Carrington

*In his* A Subaltern's War, *published under the pseudonym Charles Edmunds in 1928.*

The western and southern slopes of the village [Orvillers] had been comparatively little shelled; that is, a little grass had still room to grow between the shell-holes. The village was guarded by tangle after tangle of rusty barbed wire … Among the wire lay rows of khaki figures, as they had fallen to the machine-guns on the crest, thick as the sleepers in the Green Park on a summer Sunday evening. The simile leapt to my mind … of flies on a fly paper. . . The flies were buzzing obscenely over the damp earth; morbid scarlet poppies grew scantily among the white chalk mounds; the air was tainted with rank explosives and the sickly stench of corruption.

> Among the wire lay rows of khaki figures …

*Quoted in* The Somme Then and Now, *John Giles; rev. ed. published by Battle of Britain Prints International Ltd, 1986.*

## Siegfried Sassoon, poet
*A rifleman with the London Rifle Brigade.*

As I stepped over one of the Germans an impulse made me lift him up from the miserable ditch. Propped up against the bank, his blonde face was undisfigured, except by the mud which I wiped from his eyes and mouth with my sleeve. He'd evidently been killed while digging, for his tunic was knotted about his shoulders. He didn't look to be more than eighteen... Perhaps I had some dim sense of the futility which had put an end to this good-looking youth. Anyhow I hadn't expected the Battle of the Somme to be quite like this...

## Propped up against the bank, his blonde face was undisfigured . . .

*From* Memoirs of an Infantry Officer, *Faber and Faber, 1930.*

## Lieutenant-Colonel Graham Seton Hutchinson D.S.O.
Warrior, *published by Hutchinson and Co. (Publishers) Ltd, 1932*

I was borne to a Casualty Clearing Station but I had to wait my turn for a vacant bed. Wounded were being cleared as fast as surgeons in their shirt-sleeves could accomplish their work. But speedy as were the butchers, death was faster still and left ample space for incomers. British and Germans were treated alike; and beside me lay a young Bavarian, his chin still hairless, one of the Alpine Corps, from mountains I knew and loved, with a shattered thigh and other grievous injuries... While others groaned, and some shrieked with agony, he never uttered a sound. Only when night fell and the lamps were lighted did he begin to whimper quietly... He was crying like a child, so I touched his hand, and he held on. I think that made his passage easier, for he sighed and smiled at me, and a little later he slept. Then they took the body away.

## While others groaned, and some shrieked with agony, he never uttered a sound.

*Quoted in* The Somme Then and Now, *John Giles; rev. ed. published by Battle of Britain Prints International Ltd, 1986.*

## Stanley Spencer, artist

*Spencer, who enlisted with the Royal Army Medical Corps in 1915, recalls the scene at a dressing station in Macedonia in September 1916, to which wounded were brought by mule-drawn stretchers. The scene became the basis of his great painting,* Travoys with Wounded Soldiers Arriving at a Dressing Station at Smol, Macedonia *(1919).*

I was standing a little way from the old Greek church, which was used as a dressing station and operating theatre, and coming there were rows of travoys with wounded and limbers crammed full of wounded men. One would have thought that the scene was a sordid one, a terrible scene... but I felt there was a grandeur... all those wounded men were calm and at peace with everything, so that pain seemed a small thing with them. I felt there was a spiritual ascendancy over everything.

... all those wounded men were calm and at peace with everything ...

## Walter Tull of the 17th Middlesex Regiment (Football)

*In a letter to his brother in Scotland, Walter Tull describes a long day at work. A player with Tottenham Hotspur before the war, Second Lieutenant Tull, the first black officer in the British Army, was killed in an attack on German trenches at Favreuil on 24 March 1918.*

*Officers' Rest House,*
*France,*

*Aug. 10th 1917*

Dear Eddie,

I'm once more enjoying life some miles from the front line & if that jade 'rumour' doesn't err, we shall be a few miles still further away by this time next week. . .

I joined the Battalion on Saturday when they came back from the line & was at once posted to 'D' Coy. On Monday at noon my Coy. Commdr. detailed me to go up and inspect the position of [the] trench 'D' Coy. were to hold as we were to go up that night.

Three other Subs. & myself started off about 1.30 but Fritz was shelling the back areas like a demon & after dodging about from trench to trench we got fed up & struck across country. We were lucky, & got to a tunnel which would help us on our way considerably. Unfortunately the outlet was flooded & we got soaked up to our hips, but H2O is less dangerous than shrapnel or H.E. From the flooded place we had to [go] along a track knee deep in mud, but Fritz let us alone & we reached retired HQ safely, where the Adjt. of the Batt. to be relieved made us welcome and gave us tea. From there our way lay across open ground formerly no man's land, now one mass of shell holes. It was impossible to proceed in a straight line anywhere for more than one or two yards. Our guide did his best, & after being on our way about five hours from the time we left Camp, we reached our destination, a distance of about 3 miles taking direct line. My Coy. arrived soon after 1 a.m. & then it was informed it would not be wanted. You can guess I wasn't long in getting a move on, but by the time I was back in the tunnel I was well knocked & begged a seat amongst some R.E. Signallers. I found they were all from Scotland. Didn't Glasgow Corporation form a Coy.?...They

refreshed me with a good tot of rum, & I sat talking until nearly 5 a.m. when I pushed on for the nearest village. I must have been within 200 yards of the place when I very nearly collapsed, & suddenly remembered I'd had nothing to eat since lunch, about 17 hours since. A Y.M.C.A. canteen was my salvation.

Fritz was shelling the back areas like a demon . . .

*This letter is in the 'Walter Tull' file in the Documents Department of the Imperial War Museum.*

### Herbert Innel Minchin

*Served with the Machine Gun Corps, 54th Battalion, 34th Division in France and Belgium.*

[Our base] was Camiers, which was about five kilometres from Boulogne, on the sea coast. It was a huge camp, quite on up-to-date lines. It was here that I saw the First Expeditionary Force Canteen. Everything possible could be procured, and the best of everything, including white bread which we had not seen for months. Didn't we make a meal of it. But there was plenty of food in the camp. In fact, we used to get sufficient left over from tea to make good suppers. I had half a pound of cheese from the tea-table on many occasions, and by bringing some bread from the canteen we were well away.

> Everything possible could be procured, and the best of everything, including white bread ...

*From document Minchin H. I., 06/55/1 in the Documents Department of the Imperial War Museum.*

## Captain Edward Pennell, Royal Flying Corps

*Describes his treatment after being forced to crash-land his plane in a field after a bombing raid deep behind enemy lines in 1917.*

[After my forced landing] the French officers left one of their party to look after the remains of my machine [and they] took me to their camp where I was interrogated by their Commanding Officer. I had no identity papers of any sort, for we had to leave all things that might be useful to the enemy behind. My maps and plan of the Hirson target I had already thrown into the fire of my machine. . .

The French C.O. invited me to his Officer's Mess, where I was treated as a VIP. I was served with excellent coffee, cakes and biscuits, and introduced to a very nice wash-room in the beautiful house which this army regiment used as their Officer's Headquarters.

A wash and brush-up helped to revive my spirits, and on returning to the Mess I was given an invitation to lunch. By this time, more officers had arrived, and a few of them could speak English, which enabled me to carry on a fairly easy conversation with them, for my knowledge of the French language had been sadly neglected.

If all the drinks offered me had been accepted, I am afraid they would have had to carry me into lunch. Drinking and flying do not go well together, if one wants to live!

*From document Captain E. R. Pennell, P427 in the Documents Department of the Imperial War Museum.*

## Corporal R. G. Plint, 26th Royal Fusiliers, 'Bankers' Battalion

*describes a train journey from the Western Front to the Italian lines at Piave in November 1917. Four months later he made the return journey, detraining at Achiet-le-Grand, where 'the guns were going and over the landscape the troops were moving up to the line – we were back'.*

We awoke to find ourselves standing in a small station with palm trees growing about and the blue Mediterranean beyond. Our [train] journey that day to Genoa was almost triumphal as we passed through the towns of the Riviera. The local English residents and others turned out to greet us; canteens were provided at several stations but no payment expected; drinks, flowers and fruit were all given to us, service p.c.s [postcards] handed round and collected afterwards for transmission home. All

very jolly. Some of the cards were hand-stamped 'Wellcome old merry Fellows', others had printed 'To the Valient English brothers Our Welcome'; at Savona a broadsheet was handed to us from a Mayor stating that 'just as he had welcomed the ship-wrecked troops from Transylvania in May to Italian Ground so he now welcomed us to fight the common enemy'.

We could, of course, have gone almost the whole way [nearly 100 miles from Gioto in the Po Valley] by train but the object was to 'show the flag' and so we foot-slogged it through villages and country towns with names that rolled off the tongue… until we arrived at the foothills of 'il Montello' which force the Piave to turn east and skirt round them on its way to the Adriatic.

… canteens were provided at several stations but no payment expected; drinks, flowers and fruit were all given to us …

*From document R. G. Plint MM, 80/19/1 in the Documents Department of the Imperial War Museum.*

## Herbert Innel Minchin

*Served with the Machine Gun Corps, 54th Battalion, 34th Division in France and Belgium.*

On April 8th [1918] about 8 o'clock in the evening, we began to notice the German shelling was livening up considerably. In fact, some of them, not small ones either, dropped either on our billet [a badly damaged school] or to the front and rear, and our windowless rooms [hung with bags to keep light out] did not seem particularly safe. Once or twice we tried to settle down but it was useless, and as there seemed to be a nasty odour from the burst shells I put my gas mask on. It was lucky that I did so, as next morning revealed. It got so hot out that we were forced to seek refuge in the cellars. And here we got a few hours' sound sleep, the last we were to have for some days. When daylight came it was to find shell-fire as heavy as before, and to realise that the majority of the men in the building had been gassed, many of them badly. One man had his body and legs badly burned by mustard gas. My respirator had saved me; the only effect the gas had on me was to take away my voice for a few days.

## ... the majority of the men had been gassed ...

*From document Minchin H. I., 06/55/1 in the Documents Department of the Imperial War Museum.*

## Corporal R. G. Plint
*26th Royal Fusiliers, 'Bankers' Battalion*

Baths usually meant a change of under-clothing. Each man had a complete change, vest, shirt, pants (long or short) and socks which he took with him and put on after the bath. The dirty garments were handed in and a clean change received in exchange. The dirty clothes were all 'stoved' in a big hot container in the hope that the heat would kill the lice and after that process washed in one of the back areas. Lice could not be avoided no matter how careful one was. I well remember when in the line with the Cameronians picking up the head-phones and seeing my first louse in one of the receivers.

'Long Johns' were a breeding ground and we got rid of them in exchange as soon as possible; vests were not bad, but the seams of the shirts were a happy hunting ground; we usually scorched them with a candle flame to burn out the fluff in which the lice laid their eggs. Sometimes the seam would go off like a tiny machine-gun!

> Lice could not be avoided no matter how careful one was.

*From document Minchin H. I., 06/55/1 in the Documents Department of the Imperial War Museum.*

## Herbert Innel Minchin

*Served with the Machine Gun Corps, 54th Battalion, 34th Division in France and Belgium.*

At 2.00 a.m. on Friday March 22 [1918, the day after the Germans began their last great offensive], we set out for Etaples, a place which the troops pronounced 'Etapps'...We remained at sidings at Etaples with thousands more, but we had a decent send-off, for early as it was, English ladies were astir with hot tea and coffee from the YMCA and similar places. These were a godsend to the troops; in some places they carried on well within range of the German guns.

...We detrained at a place called Berguette and were billeted in a barn. Here it was that I first found myself with 'company'. I did not like to be seen scratching, but soon it became common. Thenceforward they 'increased and multiplied'.

# I did not like to be seen scratching, but soon it became common!

*From document Minchin H. I., 06/55/1 in the Documents Department of the Imperial War Museum.*

## An unknown German soldier

*Of the 109th Reserve Regiment, XIV Reserve Corps, records the days of the British bombardment before the first day of the Battle of the Somme.*

Every one of us these five days has become years older. Bechtel said that in these five days he has lost ten pounds. Hunger and thirst have also contributed their share to that. Hunger would be easily borne, but the thirst made one almost mad. Luckily it rained yesterday and the water in the shell holes mixed with the yellow shell sulphur tasted as good as a bottle of beer.

> Hunger would be easily borne, but the thirst made one almost mad.

*From* Pals on the Somme 1916 *by Roni Wilkinson, published 2006 by Pen and Sword Military, Barnsley, South Yorkshire.*

## Corporal R. Chambers MM

*A stretcher bearer and regular soldier, he made almost daily notes with a stubby pencil in his small pocket diary. He was awarded the Military Medal on 30 November 1918.*

**November 1916**
19 Heavy rain
20 Relieved Somerset in front line
21 Heavy shelling, especially at night
23 Relieved by L. N. L.
24 Up again attacking triangle
25 Reserve at Beaumont Hamel
26 Relieved by Manchester, sent to Maile
27 Moved to Asteaux
30 Moved to Rubempre

> Surely the
> war's over.

**December**
13 Marched to Beauval
14 Marched to Bonniers
15 Marched to Nunes
16 Marched to Bours. Damn the marching
17 Moved to Liares. Letter from Nance [wife] at last
18 Marched to St Venant
19 Surely the war's over. We are spending two days in the same place.
21 Took over Dr's Cpl job. I think this will do me alright.
22 Marched into trenches between La Bassee and Neuve Chapelle
25 Christmas Day. Hope this is the last in France.

## January 1917

19 Just moving up ready for attack at dawn. Nerves none too good, but still keep smiling. I'd like to have the bloke who keeps firing these damn great shells into our trench. Its them that put the wind into chaps.

29 Attack came off alright at dawn. Fritz put up a terrific barrage, but we gained objective after hand to hand fighting. Good few prisoners taken. Had heaps of close shaves but my lucky star shone every time. Lots of wounded in all night. Feel done to the wide.

29 4.30 Thank God, relief at last, just in time to get clear before day-break. Marched to Arras. Had a decent wash and shave and feed at last. Feel a new man.

24 [February?] Over again and captured Beaucourt.

25 Over again, bags of wounded, hard scrapping going on. What about a relief. Damn this advancing. I want to sleep for years and years. Captured Farerneil [?]. Hell of a barrage with big stuff.

26 Division doesn't move forward today. Sleep at last.

## Damn this advancing.

*From document Chambers R., 02/5/1 in the Documents Department of the Imperial War Museum.*

## Private Frank Sumpter, London Rifle Brigade

*Recalls the camaraderie with the enemy during Christmas in the trenches.*

After the 19th December [1914] attack, we were back in the same trenches when Christmas Day came along. It was a terrible winter… The devastated landscape looked terrible in its true colours – clay and mud and broken brick – but when it was covered in snow it was beautiful. Then we heard the Germans singing 'Silent night, Holy night,' and they put up a notice saying 'Merry Christmas', so we put one up too.

    While they were singing our boys said, 'Let's join in,' so we joined in and when we started singing, they stopped. And when we stopped, they started again. So we were easing the way.

> … they put up a notice saying 'Merry Christmas', so we put one up too …

Then one German took a chance and jumped up on top of the trench and shouted out 'Happy Christmas, Tommy!'. So of course our boys said, 'If he can do it, we can do it,' and we all jumped up. A sergeant-major shouted 'Get down!' But we said, 'Shut up, Sergeant, it's Christmas time!' and we all went forward to the barbed wire....

We never said a word about the war to the Germans. We spoke about our families, about how old we were, how long we thought it would last... most of the boys stayed there the whole day and only came back in the evening. There were no shots fired... it was good to walk around.

*From a tape recording in the Imperial War Museum, in* Forgotten Voices of the Great War, *Max Arthur, Ebury Press, London, 2002.*

## John Lucy, Regular Army Officer

*His view of the Kitchener volunteer, in* There's a Devil in the Drum, *Faber, London 1938.*

He was undersized. He slouched. He was bespectacled. He wore uniform in a careless way, and he had a deadly earnestness, which effectively took the place of our cold-willed esprit de corps. He saluted awkwardly, and was very clumsy with his weapons. His marching was a pain to look at, and the talkative methods of his officers and NCOs made us blush. His childish admiration of what was left of the old army was very disarming.

> He wore uniform in a careless way, and he had a deadly earnestness ...

*Quoted in* Call-to-Arms, The British Army 1914-18, *Charles Messenger, Cassell 2006.*

# KEEPING THE HOME
# FIRES BURNING

# Keeping the Home Fires Burning

Britain's home front became a war front on 16 December 1914. From the sea eight German cruisers shelled the East Coast towns of Hartlepool, Scarborough and Whitby, causing death and destruction.

Soon, England was also being attacked from the air. Germany started sending Zeppelins over the Channel in January 1915, when two airships bombed targets in East Anglia. Four people in King's Lynn were killed during this attack, and others were killed or hurt in an increasing number of Zeppelin attacks, culminating in the first attack on London at the end of May.

At first, air raid warnings were primitive: whistle-blowing policemen or Boy Scouts on bicycles with notices back and front saying 'Take Cover' and, later, 'All Clear'. These were followed by maroons (noisy warning signal rockets) which sounded all too like an air raid. By the time, around September 1916, when the RFC's air defence of London began producing good results, including the destruction of several of Germany's new R-class 'Super Zeppelins' in October, air raids were signalled by more effective sirens.

It was not until October 1915 that the RFC was ordered to bring some of its machines for a trial period of anti-aircraft work near London. But in the one major airship attack after this, on 13/14 October, when there were 71 casualties and thousands of poundsworth of damage done, the half dozen sorties mounted by the RFC with the few aeroplanes that could be spared from the Western Front achieved very little.

After the airships came much more effective aeroplanes – Taubes and Gothas. Germany sent 53 Zeppelin raids and 57 aeroplane raids over England, mostly in the south, but also along the eastern seaboard, during the war. Some 1,400 people were killed in these raids, including 800 of London's citizens in 1917 and 1918, and 3,407 people were injured, some very seriously. These figures seem small indeed, when compared with the numbers of dead and injured in World War II. But they were nightmarish for the people of Britain – ordinary civilians had not been in the front line of battle like this before.

While the war in the air continued over the Home Front, on the ground, the war was affecting life in many ways. Causing particular distress to many families was the way in which the Army was apparently being very lax in its duty to ascertain the ages of the young men it was sending to the battle fields. By mid-1915, when thousands of boys, some as young as 14 or 15, in both the Regular Army and the Territorials had been killed or badly wounded, a growing outcry in the country led a Midlands MP, Sir Arthur Markham, to launch a year-long campaign to get under-age soldiers released from service and sent home.

Newspaper propaganda and anti-German feeling continued throughout the war, with London's daily newspapers well to the fore in the attack on Germany. There were no Germans in the popular press, only savage and uncivilised Huns. Again and again, happenings, originally nothing exceptional in warfare, took on a terrible aspect when written up in the daily papers.

The Royal Family, embarrassed by their very Germanic Saxe-Coburg-Gotha surname (inherited from that fine German, Prince Albert), changed it to the much more patriotic and British-sounding 'Windsor'; their Battenberg cousins became 'Mountbatten'. They did a great deal of fund-raising, especially for medical and nursing equipment to be sent to the Front. Two of George V's sons did war service, Edward, Prince of Wales, with the Army in France (where, to his own frustration, he was kept well away from the front line, but was still often to be seen getting around on a bicycle) and Albert, Duke of York (later George VI), in the Navy, where he served as a midshipman. The king's daughter, Princess Mary, launched a fund in October 1914 to send a Christmas present to 'every sailor afloat and every soldier on the front' that resulted in 355,000 Princess Mary Gift Boxes being sent to the forces abroad that Christmas.

Like newspapers, the film industry, both in America and in Britain, played a leading role in the dissemination of anti-German propaganda. Picture palaces did very good business indeed during the Great War, with soldiers on leave and their families filling every seat, watching films such as Cecil B. de Mille's *The Little German*, starring Mary Pickford. A 1916 British film was a very different affair. This was the documentary *The Battle of the Somme* which, although it could not convey the blood-drenched fiasco that the Somme really was, provided cinema-goers with a very affecting and eloquent account of the realities of trench warfare.

## Norman Collins

*Seventeen-year-old apprentice witnessing the German naval attack on Hartlepool on 16 December 1914.*

I was still eating [breakfast] when a terrific explosion rocked the house. We had two shore batteries sited nearby and during normal firing practice we received prior notice to open our windows to avoid the glass being shattered by the guns' blast. This was no normal firing practice, for following the inferno of noise there came a reek of high explosive. I didn't know what had happened so I rushed outside. Clouds of brick dust and smoke eddied around me before I ran towards the promenade, which was only fifty yards away. On the seafront, half left, were three huge grey German ships, blazing away, and in the dull light of a winter's morning it was like looking into a furnace. At first I didn't understand the screeching noise that passed over my head like huge pencils on a slate, and then I realised they were shells... Each ship had about eight large guns, so that there were about twenty-four large shells being fired on the town at any one time... It was an amazing sight to watch broadsides from battle cruisers as close as that.

*From* All Quiet on the Home Front, *Richard van Emden and Steve Humphries, Headline Book Publishing, 2004.*

## Victor McArdell

*Recalls the intensity of anti-German feeling in London's East End in 1915.*

I was a boy, seven years of age, when the war broke out and lived at East Ham, a suburb on the fringes of the East End of London, and well remember the Zeppelin raids, the first of which occurred in the Spring of 1915. I recall the surprise and shock of my parents and neighbours and the brave face that my brothers and I put on to cover our fears and beating hearts. But never once did I witness panic or defeatism, on the contrary, there was an intensification of bitterness and hatred towards the Germans. . .

The [Zeppelin] raids did lead to an outbreak of spy-mania and I remember a gentle, benign, elderly German barber, who lived in the same road, being suspected of signalling to the raiders with a flash lamp. Absolute nonsense, of course. He was obliged eventually to move from the neighbourhood; in view of his advanced age the authorities never considered him a sufficient risk to intern.

On another occasion an angry crowd gathered outside a house – the occupants of which, according to rumour, were German spies and furthermore someone had looked through the letter-box and had seen saucers of blood in the hallway. Due largely to government propaganda, no enormity, committed by a German, was too great for the people to believe.

*Document file, Letters Describing Zeppelin Raids, First World War, Misc. 276, Item 3728, in the Documents Department of the Imperial War Museum.*

## Vera Brittain, writer and pacifist

*Writes to her fiancé, Roland Leighton, serving on the Western Front. Less than two months later, Roland was dead, shot by a German sniper.*

FIRST LONDON GENERAL HOSPITAL, 30 OCTOBER 1915
I went into Westminster Abbey for a few minutes. The evening service (which is now held in the afternoon because of Zeppelins) was going on. The music seemed to swell & thrill & lose itself in the great arches of the roof, and everything beneath the window was shadow, dimly lit by dusky gleams of sun. I thought of the last time I was in London – when you were here, & to my great astonishment found tears in my eyes when the dream faded. After all, it must be a great inspiration to be you – and such as you. I felt this afternoon that I would gladly work & fight & die, if I could only do one little bit towards saving this beauty from destruction. And that is what You are doing – & have been doing for seven long and weary months.

> . . . if I could only do one little bit towards saving this beauty from destruction.

*In* Letters from a Lost Generation, *edited by Alan Bishop and Mark Bostridge, p/b edition Virago Books, 2008.*

## Tube Camps

*The* Daily Mail, *Tuesday 25 September 1917, describes a scene that, in the next war, would become all too familiar.*

FAMILY PARTIES AND COMIC SONGS
The happiest people in London were those who at the first alarm were able to dive down into the Tube railways. Thousands took refuge there and sat out the raid in complete serenity, knowing that they would be undisturbed by either sight or sound of what might be happening overhead. At the Oxford Circus, Tottenham Court Road and Museum stations of the Central London Railway whole families from the Soho district and its environs were camping down on the platforms or in the lower passages. They had brought rugs and mats and spread them out, and father, mother, and in some cases three or four small children, were seated, smiling broadly at their great good fortune.

…The men calmed the fears of the women, and after a time stolid British silence was the prevailing note among the people. Popular songs were started, and soon the stations were echoing to rollicking choruses, while some of the more youthful in the crowd performed step dances to lighten the time.

Thousands took refuge there and sat out the raid in complete serenity …

## J. E. T. Willis

*Remembers in 1973 his reactions to First World War air-raids over London.*

I was born January 1908 which makes my age during that period [World War I] six to ten years but memories even at this length of time are extremely vivid. I lived in South East London which was the limit that the German planes could reach at that time and mostly the raids took place on clear moonlit nights as the pilots could then see their targets and just heave the bombs over the side of the cock-pit.

I remember the Saturday morning daylight raid very clearly as at that time I was in the street with my friend playing marbles. Suddenly a loud salvo of anti-aircraft fire, we looked up and my elder brother counted 32 planes (Taubs I think) floating about the sky.

Searchlights played a big part in the 'nightly show' as we called it and to see a plane caught in the lights was something to remember and most exciting, though I don't believe anybody knew whether [the aeroplane] was one of theirs or ours.

We boys spent a long time of our leisure hours looking for bits of shrapnel or bomb splinters in the wooden blocks of the roads and good specimens were very valuable as swapping material.

On the whole I believe the raids did not do much material damage but were aimed at the morale of the population...

*Document file* Letters Describing Zeppelin Raids, First World War, *Misc. 276, Item 3728, in the Documents Department of the Imperial War Museum.*

## Mrs Lydia Peile

*Living in a nursing home in Margate, describes in her diary in 1916 her first sighting of a Zeppelin.*

AUGUST 1

We had a very disturbed night [in Margate] last night, – at last I have had my wish and seen a Zeppelin. I was just going to get into bed when I heard the 'All Out' shouted from Headquarters to the machine gun men. They made an awful noise and woke Misoné up, who immediately got up and put her head out of the window. Rebie also came in, but as we could hear nothing we all retired to our beds… at about 11.30 we were just dropping off to sleep, when I heard a gun…

We…heard the Zeppelin approaching so I suggested we should go downstairs…

We opened the front door & we could see searchlights moving about and there was one from a ship at sea – the firing had rather slackened but we could see isolated shells bursting. The noise of the engine got louder so we came inside, not knowing where it was. After a few minutes we went out again. I went out first and saw the Zeppelin and I persuaded Rebie & Misoné to come out too, as they would regret it all their lives [if they didn't]. Eventually we spotted the Zeppelin going towards Westgate… There was no searchlight on the Zepp, & it looked just a small, dark object going along. We then lost

*Document file Mrs Lydia Peile, 94/2/1, in the Documents Department of the Imperial War Museum.*

KEEPING THE HOME FIRES BURNING

sight of it, but a few minutes afterwards we saw it again (or another) going in the opposite direction towards Kingsgate – this time the searchlights got on to it & we saw it splendidly. It looked just like a silver cigar. We had to come in again when the guns started firing at it, but we went out again when it had gone further and still could see it. Most of the shells were bursting far below it, but one seemed to go nearer the mark & for a few seconds it looked as if the Zeppelin almost stopped, & I feared it was going to start dropping its bombs. However, it went on again & then we saw it diving and after that we lost sight of it. The firing gradually ceased & all was quiet except for the buzz of an aeroplane. Then we saw a big red light in the sky, & I believe our aeroplanes show such a light in case they should be mistaken for the enemy.

... for a few seconds it looked as if the Zeppelin had almost stopped, and I feared it was going to start dropping its bombs.

## John Gielgud, actor

*Recalls an early theatrical experience.*

# The theatre was full of khaki and blue ...

One of my earliest theatrical memories is seeing Oscar Asche in Chu-Chin-Chow… I was overwhelmed by the production, which fulfilled my most cherished pictorial enthusiasms, first inspired by the drawings of Edmund Dulac, Arthur Rackham and Kay Nielsen…

One effect I remember particularly was the opening procession of servants carrying big bowls of food, like a Veronese painting; and there were donkeys and camels and beautiful girls in yashmaks. Asche himself played the wicked king of the robbers and sported gold fingernails, while his wife, Lily Brayton wore an enormous fuzzy black wig and transparent Oriental draperies.

It was wartime and the troops, home on leave from the trenches, adored Chu-Chin-Chow. The theatre was full of khaki and blue, and there was one scene that never failed to bring the house down. It was set in the slave-market and featured tiers of beautiful girls with very little on.

*From* An Actor and His Time, *John Gielgud, Sidgwick & Jackson, 1979*

## Mr G. Davies

*Recalled in 1973 his boyhood delight in going to the cinema in England during World War I.*

The audience was alarmed by the sound of gunfire. The film was stopped and a flash put on the screen which read: 'Patrons should not leave their seats. The building is bombproof. We built it ourselves so we know.' So the audience stayed and the film went on.

The film was a burlesque, starring 'Pimple'(Fred Evans) who was at that time an equal rival with Charles Chaplin. The title was *Pimple's Night Out!* showing how the rascal, who had joined the special air raid police, blew out and burst a large paper bag in a back room and then rushed in to tell his wife that the Zeppelins were here and he must be off, on 'duty'.

## 'Patrons should not leave their seats. The building is bombproof.'

*Document file, Letters Describing Zeppelin Raids, First World War, Misc. 276, Item 3728, in the Documents Department of the Imperial War Museum.*

## Mr G. Davies

*Recalled in 1973 the Zeppelin raids on London during his boyhood.*

In those days most London street lighting was by gas or arc-light. Black-out was easy for the arc lit main streets, but most back streets were hand lit and an army of lamplighters with poles were employed to walk the streets. So total blackout sometimes came after the raid was over. Then came the search by boys for bomb and shell splinters and front door gossip. As I passed one group I heard a man scaring the women with 'it's not the bombs you have to be afraid of, its these arrows they drop that comes down and pins you to the pavement.' (There had been a press story of anti-personnel darts.)

Air raids were still a novelty and the potential danger was anyone's guess, so public reaction was totally different to that in the Second World War. At first, Parliament could not even make up its mind to sanction air raid warnings, and when they did, it was in the form of noisy maroons with a shattering bang and scarlet flare, which were mistaken by many for the raid itself, and so did not make for damping panic. . .

The Zeppelins in their short period of supremacy held a terror somewhat analogous to the V.2s of the second war, in their facility of shutting off engines and floating silently inside a

So total black-out sometimes came after the raid was over. Then came the search by boys for bomb and shell splinters and front door gossip.

drifting cloud, with an observation chamber suspended by cable at the lower fringe of the cloud, in telephone communication with the ship.

During this period no restaurant keeper would be surprised if you ordered 'Zepp and a portion of clouds.' He would serve you without question with sausage and mashed potatoes.

*Document file, Letters Describing Zeppelin Raids, First World War, Misc. 276, Item 3728, in Documents Department of the Imperial War Museum. Letters were written to Dr. Ralph N. Traxler Jnr, University of South Alabama, Mobile, Alabama 36688, USA, in response to letter he inserted in several UK newspapers in 1973.*

## Mrs Lydia Peile of Margate

*Records in her diary one of the two air raids made on England on 22 August 1916. The one she experienced was an attack by a squadron of Gotha aeroplanes on the Kent coast, in which 11 people were killed and 13 wounded, including patients in Chatham Hospital. The second air raid of the day was made by airships on the coast of Yorkshire. The damage there was slight.*

**Wednesday, 22 August**

We had an awful air raid again this morning. To begin with, I didn't sleep well last night owing to some heavy firing a long way off which kept on rattling the doors & windows. Misoné & I started out early to do our shopping. The last shop I went to was Bobby's. I had just left it & was wheeling Misoné towards home when we saw a lot of people gazing skywards. On looking up too, we saw 3 or 4 aeroplanes at good height up & we were all very suspicious of them. At that moment I heard a funny sort of noise, I thought to myself 'That's the Queen's Hotel siren trying to start off' and in a few seconds it blazed forth.

Everyone started going for shelter & I decided to run back to Bobby's, as it was nearer than going home. Another spinal chair with a man in it was just going in & so we skipped in after him, chair as well. Mr Bobby called out to people in the streets to come inside quickly if they wanted to as he had to lock the doors... Misoné got out of her chair, & we went down below where all the employees were sent. We knew a lot of the latter and they were so nice and kind to M. We had a box to sit on. All was quiet at first, but after about ten minutes, viz. at 10.25 a.m. the first guns began & so we knew we were in for it. . .

The guns made a fearful noise but we could hear the hum of many aeroplanes. Then we heard the first bomb, fairly near, & then came a terrible whistling through the air, & we realised that an aerial torpedo was coming down, & it sounded so near that we guessed it would fall unpleasantly close. . . Then came the crash and we breathed once more. Several more bombs were dropped quite near, & then came a mighty cheer from some soldiers outside & a lot of the girls, heedless of flying bits of shell, tore up the iron staircase, & then we heard them cheering too. They returned a few seconds later & said they had seen three aeroplanes falling down, two of them in flames. We all cheered too, and it bucked us up.

. . .they had seen three aeroplanes falling down, two of them in flames.

*Document file Mrs Lydia Peile, 94/2/1, in the Documents Department of the Imperial War Museum.*

## Edward Brittain to his sister Vera

# A foolish woman came out into the road and therefore received some shrapnel in one eye from one of our own guns . . .

The night of the day you left London [Vera Brittain sailed for Malta on 22 September 1916] the Zepps dropped 4 bombs on Purley somewhere up that hill where we walked one afternoon when I was still bad. Only about 600 yards from the house but it did no damage.

A foolish woman came out into the road and therefore received some shrapnel in one eye from one of our own guns but otherwise there was no damage except windows and a pillar box...

*In* Letters from a Lost Generation, *edited by Alan Bishop and Mark Bostridge, p/b edition Virago Books, 2008.*

# THE MACHINERY OF
# MODERN WARFARE

# The Machinery of Modern Warfare

The First World War was the proving ground for much of the weaponry of twentieth-century warfare. Tanks, fighter and bomber aircraft, machine guns, and trench mortars (designed initially to counter the deadly effectiveness of the German *Minenwerfer* – 'minnies' to the men in the British trenches) all became major elements in modern warfare during the Great War. But it was the transformation of the nature of artillery, much of it occurring in the decade or so before 1914, that ensured that in this war gunners, rather than infantry, were the most important men on the battlefield.

By 1914, the armies of Europe had quick-firing field guns using shells in cartridge cases, able to carry, as well as high explosive, various types of gas and shrapnel; and they had guns that did not need to be re-aimed after each firing because they were designed to absorb recoil. As for heavy guns, which the Germans, in particular, had been experimenting with because they knew that in the all-too-likely event of a war, they would have to deal with the strong fortifications of Belgium and France, they were well suited to the static, entrenched warfare of World War I. They could be set up in more-or-less permanent positions a good distance – ten miles or so – from the front line, making gunners safe from machine-gun fire and allowing the guns to be fired over the heads of their own infantry. These delivered hugely destructive bombardments combining carefully orchestrated elements of artillery – the 'Firewaltz' of German artillery tacticians – on enemy troops, fortifications and, of course, on the ground in front of them.

A much lighter gun, which could be carried, if necessary, though not without considerable difficulty, by one or two men, was the machine gun. Two decisions of November 1914 attest to the value the military men placed on the machine gun. First, after the first Battle of Ypres, was the establishment of a machine gun school at Camiers, France. Second, was the formation of the Motor Machine Gun Service (MMGS), intended to provide very mobile machine-gun detachments. The first such detachments, organised in batteries of eighteen gun/motorcycle combinations, arrived in France at the

end of 1914. Some 25 machine-gun batteries were eventually formed, at least two of them in India.

Then there was the tank, able, in theory at least, to move indomitably over the most difficult battlefield. While the Germans were in the forefront of heavy artillery developments, it was the British who first unleashed the tank on to the battlefield. The development of the tank was an initiative of Winston Churchill who, when he was First Lord of the Admiralty, in late 1914 allotted funds for research into the development of a 'land battleship'. Experiments, with early ones based on a cross-country tractor, and trials were carried out in great secrecy, so that when the tank eventually made its first appearance on the battlefield, it caught the Germans – and Allied troops, too – entirely by surprise.

Thirty-six Mark I tanks took part in the Battle of Flers-Coucelette, during the Battle of the Somme, on 15 September 1916. This first version of the tank weighed 28 tons, was 26 feet 5 inches long, and had a top speed on level ground of three and a half miles an hour. It carried a crew of eight, came in two types – a 'male' tank which had two Hotchkiss 6-pounder quick-firing guns and several machine guns, and a 'female' type which had only machine guns – and had a single wheel at the back which was intended to make it more manoeuvrable, but which, in fact, made it less so and was soon abandoned.

Four of the tanks that went into battle on that historic day made it as far as Flers, and one was observed by a British spotter plane actually entering the village and lurching ponderously up the main street with its machine guns firing, and surrounded by cheering infantry. The report written by the spotter plane's pilot eventually reached the British press, which hailed this introduction of an entirely new weapon of war with acclaim.

Although the tank's first appearance was certainly spectacular, it was too slow, unwieldy and all too likely to get bogged down in the Flanders mud to be very useful in World War I. Continuing experiments and redesigns made them more effective as the war went on: a massed tank attack took the Germans entirely by surprise at the Battle of Cambrai in November 1917. And the Americans used them to some effect on the first day of the Meuse-Argonne offensive in 1918, when a very forceful young officer called George S. Patton led his tankers from the front, rallying infantrymen around him as he went. A severe wound that day ended Patton's war, but not his enthusiasm for the tank, as his role as a general in the Second World War well demonstrated. By the end of the 1930s the tank had become a very effective weapon indeed.

Infinitely more effective, both in the short term and the long, however, was the aeroplane. Starting the war as part of a Corps – the Royal Flying Corps – commanded by officers of the British Army, the aeroplane had become, by the war's end, the main machine of an independent service, the Royal Air Force. The RAF was created on 1 April 1918 out of the merging of the RFC and the RNAS, the Royal Navy's air arm. At first, the aeroplane's greatest use was in reconnaissance, but it soon became hugely valuable as a bomber, destroying enemy supply dumps far behind the Front Line as well as the trenches and troops in them.

## Private Lance Cattermole

*21st Infantry Battalion of the Canadian Expeditionary Force 1916.*

We had recently been issued with the short Lee-Enfield rifle which we were delighted with, it being so much lighter than the heavy and long Canadian Ross rifle which, although excellent as a target rifle, with its aperture sight, was no good in the muddy trenches where this sight became clogged.

Furthermore, when rapid fire was used, the bolt jammed and had to be kicked back by the foot in order to open the breech.

> . . . the Lee-Enfield rifle . . . we were delighted with . . . being so much lighter.

*From document Cattermole L. ROI, 92/26/1 in the Documents Department of the Imperial War Museum.*

## Dick Trafford
*A minor who enlisted at the age of 15.*

We were going up in the early hours of the morning. It was dark and we passed through a battery of guns just as it opened up to start the final bombardment for the attack. I was near one of the guns and as it fired the noise burst my eardrum, blood squirting out of it, and I was deaf straight away. The sergeant took one of the little dressings we always carried in case we were wounded and packed my ear with cotton wool to plug it … we were expecting to go over the top in an hour or two, so I would have to go over the top with my ear already wounded. I wasn't allowed to turn back. There was only one way – forward.

I was near one of the guns and as it fired the noise burst my eardrum, blood squirting out of it …

*Quoted in* Boy Soldiers of the Great War, *Richard van Emden, Headline Book Publishing, 2006.*

## W. F. Chapman, stretcher-bearer
*Recalls the German front line in 1916.*

I have never seen anything quite so bad as the German front line on 15th September [1916]. The trench was full of dead, mostly apparently killed by concussion, and you could not move along the line without walking over the dead bodies. A British tank was ditched in the Jerry front trench.

I was one of the regimental stretcher-bearers at the time and I can distinctly remember the tank going through Flers and moving towards the village pump with a group of stretcher-bearers close behind. Other soldiers were following and they certainly appeared to be happy although I cannot recall whether they were cheering. I was there all day, from the time we went over the top until about 5 p.m.

> The trench was full of dead, mostly apparently killed by concussion . . .

*Quoted in* The Somme Then and Now, *John Giles; originally published by Bailey Brothers and Swinfen, 1977, rev. ed. published by Battle of Britain Prints International Ltd, 1986.*

## Battery Sergeant-Major Pegler, 24th Division Artillery
*Extracts from his diary of the war.*

### 6th September

We withdrew our guns today for a short rest and a general overhaul. In the month that the 24th Division Artillery has been in action on the Somme, my battery has fired 17,342 rounds and the Divisional Artillery has had 25 officer casualties with a proportionate number of fallen NCOs and men. We had one officer Lieut Westerberg (a Dane not a Boche) killed this morning just before we came out.

### 7th September

This morning General Philpotts, Comdg the Artillery of the 24th Division conveyed to us the congratulations of the Guards Division and the 20th Division. The General Officer Commanding the Guards Division said that 'The Artillery of the 24th Division have these last few days put up the most magnificent shooting I have ever seen, and their barrages were walls of fire which nothing could penetrate and live, and the Officers and men of the Guards Division ask for nothing better than to be covered by the gunners of the 24th Division.' Some 'reference' that.

*Document file Pegler D. H. Captain 82/7/1, in the Documents Department of the Imperial War Museum.*

## Regimental Sergeant Major J. H. Price DCM, Shropshire LI

It was September 15th 1916, we had taken up our positions close to Delville Wood. During the night my C. O. came to see if the men had settled down for some rest. He then told me that in the attack the next morning we would have the help of a new weapon. I asked what form this would take and he said we would have the help of three tanks, and I asked him: - 'Did the General think we would be running short of water?' He replied that they were not water tanks [but ones] that held three or four men and fired machine guns and small calibre artillery weapons. Our attack was to be made on the villages of Flers and Gueudecourt...

About 4.00 a.m. our guns, of all descriptions, opened up, and it was like hell on earth. The Germans soon started replying to our bombardment and for the next two hours this continued. . . It was 6.00 a.m on the 15th September when we left our trenches and went forward, round to the east of Delville Wood, and there we saw the first tank, spitting bullets from the top of it. We had never seen anything like it before, and I think it attracted more of our attention than the enemy... It certainly looked a monster, and it is a job for me to explain its shape, and I can only say it had huge caterpillar tracks and a large wheel behind. It went forward rather slowly and I should think it must have struck terror into many of the enemy... [By about] mid-day... things had quietened down somewhat. Two of our tanks were out of action, one by fire, and the other, I think, by having the large wheel damaged and this I was told affected the steering. But the third tank did wonderful work, capturing Flers almost on its own... A successful day on the whole, but [if] we had had another forty or fifty tanks the war would have ended that year.

A successful day on the whole, but if we had had another forty or fifty tanks the war would have ended that year.

*Document file Price J. H. DCM, 82/22/11 in the Documents Department of the Imperial War Museum.*

## Private Lance Cattermole

*21st Infantry Battalion of the Canadian Expeditionary Force 1916*

# . . . a tin of bully beef, hard tack, cheese etc . . .

In the advance, we were wearing what had come to be called 'Fighting Kit', that is the big pack was replaced on the back by the haversack, normally worn on the left side over the bayonet scabbard. This made movement much easier than the old Full marching order which troops had been wearing into battle. We carried an extra issue of ammunition in a cotton bandolier, and a spare Mills bomb in each side pocket. In addition, our iron ration, consisting of a tin of bully beef, hard tack, cheese etc., was slung at our left side in a white cotton bag.

Each man had been issued with a bright yellow, triangular pennant. This was carried in our haversack... and was pulled out before 'going over', so that it lay on the back of the haversack, forming a sort of distinctive label that could be seen by our spotter planes which hovered over us during the advance.

*From document Cattermole L. ROI , 92/26/1 in the Documents Department of the Imperial War Museum.*

## Herbert Innel Minchin

*Served with the machine gun corps of 54th Battalion, 34th Division, in France and Belgium.*

The training for the machine gun corps is very trying and very hard, but it proved more interesting than any I have yet been in. There was much carrying to do and heavy work which explained why only fit men were picked for the Corps. The Vickers gun itself when filled with water weighs 40lb; then there is the heavy tripod which has to be carried by one leg over each shoulder, and the trail leg down the back. That is two men's work, and it was impossible to carry them far without a rest. Others carried the spare parts box and belt boxes, each carrying one belt with 200 rounds of ammunition, so that a machine section on the move, when no transport was possible, were in for a good time, especially when equipped in full marching order.

Eight weeks was the time allowed at this period to become an expert or efficient machine gunner, but whether one was efficient or not made no difference ultimately.

> . . . only fit men were picked for the Corps.

*From document Minchin H. I., 06/55/1 in the Documents Department of the Imperial War Museum.*

## Captain E. R. Pennell

*The engine of Captain Pennell's plane failed during a bombing mission to a railway junction at Hirson, about 60 miles over the enemy lines, in 1917.*

To my alarm my engine [a 160 h.p. Beardmore engine fitted to a Jumbo Martynside plane] was now beginning to give me trouble. The revs were dropping, and I had great difficulty keeping up with the formation... By now I began to lose height and eventually I was down to cloud level. Flying through an opening my first thought was to find out where I was, but this was hopeless. Setting my machine by my compass due west, and nursing my engine all the time... I hoped and prayed that I would eventually reach the other side of the lines...

I looked about for a good open field ahead, and made preparations to put the machine down. The field I chose was alongside a large wood and luckily was nice and level. Gliding in, I made a good landing and on coming to rest I undid my safety belt and got out of my machine, taking my revolver and Verys pistol (this was used for firing the signal lights) with me. To my horror I was astounded to see German soldiers coming out of the wood.

My reaction was swift. I shot up my petrol tank and fired a Verys light into it. The result was a terrific blaze of petrol and the machine was soon well alight. The German soldiers stood

# Flying through an opening my first thought was to find out where I was . . .

outside the wood and watched the fire burn and to my surprise took no action to arrest me.

A short while after, a car came up a lane nearby and out ran four French Army officers. They tried to extinguish the flames, shouting ... as they did so, 'Are there any 'Bombeys' with the machine?'

My lovely plane, to which I had become so attached, and which I had burned, was no more. I felt like weeping. We had done so many bomb raids together, and it had never let me down before. Alas that my hand should destroy it. But I had only carried out the orders which were given to pilots, 'that the first thing on landing in enemy territory was to destroy our machine.'

[One of the French officers] told me that the German soldiers in the wood were prisoners-of-war working in the wood cutting down trees. As they were facing me at the time of their exit from the wood, I did not notice the patches of different colours which had been sewn into the backs of their uniforms – the usual practice to make prisoners-of-war easily identifiable.

*From document Captain E. R. Pennell P427 in the Documents Department of the Imperial War Museum.*

## Rory Macleod

*Recounts in his unpublished memoirs the firing of a home-made trench mortar by an RHA battery in the 2nd Indian Cavalry Division, Neuve Chapelle sector, March 1915.*

The barrel looked like a bit of gas piping on a stand and it fired bombs consisting of jam tins filled with high explosive and nails. The Battery intended to practise first. They formed in a shallow square around the mortar. The first three bombs were fired successfully, Wingate-Guy, a subaltern being the demonstrator and lighting the fuse. The fourth bomb exploded in the bore and killed the Major… and 13 men, and wounded about 40 others… Wingate-Guy, by some miracle, escaped injury.

> The fourth bomb exploded in the bore and killed the Major …

*Quoted in* Call to Arms: The British Army 1914-18, *Charles Messenger, Cassell, 2006.*

## Private Lance Cattermole

*Of the 21st Infantry Battalion of the Canadian Expeditionary Force discovered that not all the tanks brought up for the Battle of Flers-Courcelette on 15 September 1916 were the real thing.*

Tanks were used for the first time in modern warfare in this advance, and seven were allotted to the Canadians; unfortunately several broke down or got stuck... I have never seen it recorded, not heard it mentioned, that we used dummy tanks as well as real ones on this day. That at least one of these decoys was made I can vouch for, because I walked by its side and watched the canvas sides shake as it trundled along on wheels, drawn by one draught horse, at dusk, on the 'Flats' outside Albert two evenings before we advanced. It was headed towards the front line, which raises the question – were some of those tanks which supposedly never got off the mark really dummies, put there to confound the enemy and waste his ammunition?

## ... we used dummy tanks as well as real ones on this day.

*From document Cattermole L. ROI, 92/26/1 in the Documents Department of the Imperial War Museum.*

## Private Lance Cattermole

*Of the 21st Infantry Battalion of the Canadian Expeditionary Force describes the horrors of an attack by air.*

My platoon was in the third and last wave in the advance [on 15 September 1916] (the waves were twenty yards apart). We crawled over the top of the parapet and lined up on a broad, white tape, just discernible in the growing light, immediately in front of the trench and behind the first two waves which were already in position. It was almost zero hour. I looked at my wrist watch and saw that we had about three minutes to go. I never heard our officers' whistles to signal the advance, and I don't suppose they heard them either because of the terrific crash with which the creeping barrage opened up, exactly at 6:20 a.m.

The air over our heads was suddenly filled with the soughing and sighing, whining and screaming of thousands of shells of all calibres, making it impossible to hear anything. We stood up and I looked behind me; as far as the eye could see, from left to right, there was a sheet of flame from the hundreds of guns lined up, almost wheel to wheel, belching fire and smoke. It was an awe-inspiring sight...

An added noise made me look upwards and, through a break in the swirling morning mist, I saw one of our spotter planes, the wings golden in the rays of the rising sun against a blue sky, showing the red, white and blue roundels of the RFC. This gave me a cheerful feeling and one, too, of a thrilling excitement. I felt (a) that this was a terrific 'show' put on for my benefit, and (b) that I was an actor taking part in an epic film, both feelings at the same time – it was most extraordinary.

The air over our heads was suddenly filled with the soughing and sighing, whining and screaming of thousands of shells of all calibres . . .

*From document Cattermole L. ROI, 92/26/1 in the Documents Department of the Imperial War Museum.*

## Battery Sergeant-Major Douglas Pegler, 24th Division Artillery
*Describes in his diary the first use of tanks in warfare.*

**14 September 1916**

Last night everyone went barmy on the advent of the landships.

These are huge armoured cars built on the caterpillar system, with a prow-like front which enables them to take obstacles – they go over trenches, trees, walls (up to 4ft 6ins) with ease. They are armoured all over with $^3/_8$in [0.5cm] steel, weigh 27–30 tons and are fitted with 105hp engines. They are to advance in line in front of the infantry. Their armament is of two kinds. Some are fitted with light machine guns, and some with two quick firing six pounders and five machine guns. If they don't put the wind up Fritz he's absolutely hopeless. Their crew is one officer, one non-com and 6 gunners.

**18 September 1916**

*[in hospital, having been wounded for the third time]:*

I have forgotten the 'land crabs', the great armoured cars that took part in the battle of the fifteenth [September] – some are lying on their backs, mangled masses of twisted and broken iron, others are back in their repairing yards, all are more or less crocked but God the execution they did was awful. It struck me as I saw them … how symbolic of all war they were. Then one

# The firing gradually slackened and she lay silent, the gallant little crew burned to death each man at his gun.

saw them creeping along at about four miles an hour, taking all obstacles as they came, sputtering death with all their guns enfilading each trench as it came to it – and crushing beneath them our own dead and dying as they passed. I saw one body on a concrete parapet over which one had passed. This body was just a splash of blood and clothing about two feet [60cm] wide and perhaps an inch [2.5cm] thick, an hour before this thing had been a thinking breathing man, with life before him and loved ones awaiting him at home, probably somewhere in Scotland, for he was a kiltie.

… One [tank] had been hit by a large shell and the petrol tank pierced, she lay on her side in flames, a picture of hopelessness but every gun on the uppermost side still working with dogged determination. The firing gradually slackened and she lay silent, the gallant little crew burned to death each man at his gun.

*From document file Pegler D. H., 82/7/1 in the Documents Department of the Imperial War Museum.*

## Captain Edward Pennell, Royal Flying Corps
*Describes an early, unsuccessful attempt to use carrier pigeons as a weapon of air warfare.*

The pigeons were to be dropped behind enemy lines to assist our spies who were already working there. . . The hapless pigeons were placed in a long iron box fixed under the fuselage between the undercarriage, and controlled by the joy-stick to which was attached a Bowden wire. When the wire was pulled, it opened the bottom of the box thus ejecting the pigeons, each separated in its own compartment in the box.

The individual pigeons wore a small harness to which was attached… a small ring. The idea was that they would fly against each other and gradually drop to the ground. In

practice…[it was later found that] the birds became entangled up and were killed. . .

My particular target was near Aulnoy, some four miles to the south. I was to look out for six large hay or straw stacks in a field which also contained a herd of black and white cows. My instructions were to drop my pigeons at an altitude as low as I felt was safe, taking into consideration the fact that I had to climb again to seek cloud cover quickly and thereby avoid 'Archie' [anti-aircraft fire].

Cruising around for a while, I waited until the clouds opened up. Now was the time to go into action. I must admit

# There was timber, wire, field services etc. and all I had was a box of pigeons!

that by now I had got the wind up pretty badly. I imagined the whole of the German Air Force would be waiting to pounce on me as soon as I emerged... Surely I must be nearly over Berlin by now!

Circling around 1000 feet I searched for the stacks but they were nowhere to be seen... I began to realise that it was a thousand to one chance that a pilot could find this sort of target... On my way back, climbing steadily to get above the clouds, I looked over the side. There, below me, was a marvellous enemy dump. There was timber, wire, field services etc. and all I had was a box of pigeons!...

I arrived at my aerodrome late in the afternoon... I was met by my Flight Commander and the Army sergeant, both eager to know how I had got on. When I told my dismal story the sergeant proceeded to unload the pigeons, only to find about half of them were dead... perhaps due to the fact that they had been taken too high and remained in the cold too long.

*From document file Captain E. R. Pennell – P247, in the Documents Department of the Imperial War Museum.*

## Battery Sergeant-Major Douglas Pegler, 24th Division Artillery

*Records 'aerial activity' over the Somme in 1916 and encounters with German observation kite balloons.*

**20 August 1916**

… Artillery air fight took place over Marcourt today. A Boche was 'up' and our Antis fired at it for about twenty minutes without success, and Fritz eventually escaped in a cloud and was hidden from sight though we could hear his engine. Presently one of our planes entered the same cloud and we heard machine gun fire. Suddenly a flaming mass hurtled through the air to the ground. Fritz had made his last flight. He fell from 3000 [feet].

**21 August**

A Boche air raid took place this morning. Ten Fokkers came over and bombed us. Twenty horses were more or less seriously wounded and several killed. Three men were killed and sixteen wounded. No gun was touched.

**26 August**

Last night our anti-aircraft fire brought down four Boche machines between six and eight o'clock. To have judged from the cheering one would have thought the world gone mad. There was considerable aerial activity yesterday, at one time we could count twenty-seven English and six Boche planes in the air at one time.

**26 June**

We have just had a great buck. Four of our planes went over the Boche Lines and attacked three 'sausages' – observation kite balloons – with liquid-fire bombs and brought all three down in flames, and have now returned over us in safety. The cheering on all sides is deafening as everyone within miles must have been watching. The bombs are made some of a preparation of petrol and some of phosphorus.

**19 August**

Today we have watched a German 'sausage' brought down, it evidently got loose somewhere in Bocheland and drifted over our lines, when over Fricourt one of our Archibalds [anti-aircraft weapons] hit it in the gizzard and it immediately crumpled up and came down. Several instruments and important documents were taken from the basket.

Four of our planes went over the Boche lines and attacked three 'sausages' . . .

*From document file Pegler D. H., 82/7/1 in the Documents Department of the Imperial War Museum.*

## Gunner L. G. Whiteley, C Battery, 246 Brigade, Royal Field Artillery
*An excerpt from his diary.*

May 8 [1917] At 10.45 p.m. we had orders to 'stand to' for support for an infantry raid, and H.E., gas and smoke-shells were all to be ready for use.

At 10.50 p.m., the Trench Mortar Battery let fly with 4-inch smoke-bombs, and Jerry responded by sending up a huge wall of Verey Lights in an attempt to keep visibility open. It was like a great firework display, if it had not been so sinister. From our forward position, by the light of an almost full moon, we could plainly watch the deadly, green cloud of gas and smoke rolling slowly but surely towards the enemy line...

Mr. Colson visited us during the stand-to period, and explained that there had been no actual infantry attack that night but that the whole exercise was an experiment with a new gas bomb that the Trench Mortar Battery had been using for the first time.

The gas that it emits on impact is not deadly poisonous, but the bomb is designed to allow the gas to penetrate the enemy gas helmets, where it creates intense nausea and vomiting which, in its turn, makes the recipient pull off his helmet – and then the Mortar boys switch to the standard chlorine and phosgene bombs. Just for good measure, this is interspersed with the artillery firing 18-pounder shrapnel shells to catch anyone who has ventured into open ground to get some fresh air. Isn't war lovely?

*From document file L. G. Whiteley 06/55/1, in the Documents Department of the Imperial War Museum.*

# WOMEN GO TO WAR

# Women Go to War

In Britain in 1914, about five million women had paid jobs, most of them in domestic service, but others in the textiles and clothing industries and in shops. At the outbreak of the war, many industries that traditionally employed women were shut down because they were considered 'non-essential': about one in seven working women lost their jobs in the weeks immediately after the declaration of war. It was some time before employers began to look to women to fill the vacancies left by men who had gone to war, at first in trades considered 'suitable' for women, such as shoe-making, printing and baking.

The majority of British women, who did no paid work, the declaration of war at first seemed a signal to do little more for the war effort than to start knitting socks for soldiers. But soon it was clear that a lot more than this would be needed, and voluntary groups were set up in their hundreds to buy medical supplies and equipment, winter gloves, and even Christmas presents and other comforts for the boys at the front. Numerous well-off women, at least two duchesses among them, went to France in person, carrying all that was necessary to set up their own nursing posts, hospitals and canteens. Many women, including wives and mothers, who initially were not expected to do more than to 'keep the home fires burning', found that doing their bit during the Great War came to include some very unexpected tasks. Who among them would have thought, when they waved their husbands and sons goodbye, that welcoming them home on leave would include delousing their filthy uniforms?

Almost immediately after war was declared, many women did begin to look at serious ways of making an effort for the war, often by joining other women already in such voluntary organisations as the Voluntary Aid Detachments (VAD, founded in 1909) which, its posters said, urgently needed nursing members, cooks, kitchen maids, clerks, house-maids, ward maids, laundresses, motor drivers etc. And there were the Women's Emergency Corps, which helped women become doctors, nurses, ambulance drivers and motorcycle messengers, the Women's Defence Relief Corps, the Women's Hospital Corps, and the Women's Police Volunteers and many others.

The Women's Legion, founded in 1915, differed from the voluntary organisations in that it offered women paid work, so that it attracted many more working-class women, who could not have afforded to buy their own uniforms, as did the women who joined the voluntary organisations. The Women's Legion Military Cookery Section soon became an invaluable help in Army catering, both in Britain and in France.

Large numbers of women found themselves jobs in transport, driving and conducting buses, working as guards on the railways, and driving trucks. For others, their war work involved taking the place of men down on the farm, and helping the country produce more food than it had needed to do in peacetime, so effective was the German blockade of shipping. Although there were far fewer land girls in the Great War than in World War II, they still made a significant contribution to the war effort.

As the war went on, the demand for hugely increased amounts of armaments of all kinds, plus the ammunition for them, became unceasing. Eventually thousands of women, at first unmarried women as young as 14, but later wives and mothers, and the widows of those killed in action (for whom, given the low rate of separation or widows' allowances, extra work was essential), were all playing a vital part in keeping factory war production going in munitions factories, shell-filling factories, and in engineering, metal working and aircraft production works.

They worked long hours on day and night shifts in factories where, as the war dragged on, shifts got longer and rest breaks shorter.

For obvious reasons, munitions works were built well away from heavily populated areas, so that many women munitions workers had to be housed in hostels. The explosives the women worked with turned their hair and skins so yellow that they came to be called 'canaries'. The work was dangerous. The sound of the explosion at the Silvertown munitions factory in London in 1917, which killed 73, could be heard as far away as Cambridge. When the vast Chilwell munitions factory on the outskirts of Nottingham suffered a huge explosion in July 1918, 134 workers, many of them women, were killed.

For those women who wanted to

support the armed services, one way to do so was via nursing. The Queen Alexandra's Imperial Military Nursing Service (QAIMNS) had fewer than 500 trained nurses in August 1914; it soon could count many hundreds more in its ranks, as could the Territorial Force Nursing Service (TFNS), and numerous voluntary organisations, including the First Aid Nursing Yeomanry (FANY). FANY soon found that the purpose for which it had been formed in 1907 – galloping on to the field of battle, recovering wounded, and taking them to hospital – required a rethink; the first FANY convoy – six 'Fannies', three nurses, two orderlies and an ambulance – to go to war left England in October 1914 and had soon set up a hospital in a convent in Belgium.

Commanding officers at the front were at first very reluctant to allow women anywhere near the serious fighting: they did not want to have to take responsibility for women on the front line and many felt that, far from being of use, they would just be in the way. Many officers, just like civilians at home, had been so influenced by anti-German propaganda that they seriously felt that nurses too near the front line were quite likely to be raped by German soldiers. Such attitudes changed very quickly. In this, as in so many other areas, women's lives were changed forever by their active participation in the Great War.

## Gladys Stanford

*One of 74,000 volunteers, two-thirds of them women and girls, who had joined the near-2,500 VAD detachments established in Britain by early summer, 1914.*

We went for a whole fortnight [with a VAD attachment to a Territorial battalion annual camp in Dorset]... in May [1914] living in tents just like the men, but, of course, in a separate field...

The soldiers had exercises and mock battles and we set up a field hospital to take care of the 'wounded'. It was very interesting and great fun after practising putting splints and bandages on unwilling children and Boy Scouts. And towards the end of the fortnight we were absolutely thrilled to have a real casualty. One of the men was kicked by a horse and had his leg broken... We took it all very seriously but we hardly thought we'd be nursing the wounded in earnest before the winter set in.

> The soldiers had exercises and mock battles ...

*From* The Roses of No Man's Land, *Lyn Macdonald, Penguin Books, 1993.*

## Vera Brittain, author and feminist

*Writing to her fiancé Roland Leighton, serving on the Western Front.*

28 July 1915

I heard a day or two ago that there is a faint chance of my getting into a large London hospital as a V.A.D. The Hospital is an immense place at Camberwell (No 1, London General); it has been established I think since the beginning of the War but has recently been greatly extended & contains over a thousand beds. They have to make a necessary increase in the nursing staff & want more V.A.D.s… I should love to go there as they get all the wounded straight from the trenches and the V.A.D.s have all the minor dressing to do. Fully trained nurses are rather scarce just now and it is counted that two V.A.D.s take the place of one trained nurse (though I don't think they do really, I had no idea what a capable person a trained nurse was till I went to the Hospital). This Camberwell place is of course a Government affair and you have to sign on for six months & get paid at the immense rate of £20 a year, but you get your board and lodging free as well.

… they get all the wounded straight from the trenches …

*In* Letters From a Lost Generation, *edited by Alan Bishop and Mark Bostridge, p/b edition, Virago Press, 2008.*

## Sister J. Paterson

*One of the first civilian nursing sisters to reach the Front, describes a typical day.*

Sometimes we feed & dress [the wounds of] 200–300 a day in and out, different convoys. Sometimes we keep them a night if there is not an ambulance train to take them off; hands and feet washed & at least change their socks most of which we cut off. They are moulded to their limbs having generally been on 5, 6, 7 weeks.

You hear a whistle, then up dash ambulances one after the other, next the doors of my ward swing open (I have at present a huge hall, belonging to a Monastery) & in tumbles a dusty weary crew followed or preceded by stretcher cases. We seat them at long tables at the end, give them a bottle of stout each and cigarettes, see if any require immediate dressing, then order a piping hot meal, soup & stew & chunks of bread. Our Colonel feeds them awfully well, then we generally let them have a sleep while we attend to 'stretcher' cases. It is hard work but when you see the convoy go out you are repaid, especially if you have had them for a night. Soap here is a luxury and dear. Many thanks for the socks, they will be forwarded here with my other parcels. Please thank the ladies of your Committee & tell them how I distributed the last lot. Now the men travel in comparative luxury, motor ambulances, lovely ambulance trains – at first carts without springs and cattle trucks on straw – such a difference . . .

*Document file Sister J. Paterson, 90/10/1 in the Documents Department of the Imperial War Museum.*

## Front page of the *Daily Sketch* newspaper
## Saturday, 26 November 1915

*Written up in typical near-hysterical style, of the attack on the* Braemar Castle.
*The photograph of the nurses, all wearing their uniforms embellished with large
white collar and white cuffs, and with their nun-like white veils, shows them,
smiling happily, sitting on the deck of the ship.*

ANOTHER HUN OUTRAGE OF THE RED CROSS

There is no atrocity too vile for the Huns to encompass, no outrage of Humanity's laws too flagrant to perpetrate. Close upon the sinking of the Britannic hospital ship comes news that another stately liner, the *Braemar Castle*, bearing the sacred symbols of the Red Cross, has been 'mined or torpedoed' in the Aegean Sea. That all aboard, including homeward-bound wounded are reported saved is a mercy that does not lessen the brutality of the crime. These photographs show the *Braemar Castle* ready to leave Salonika, and types of the brave nurses who face death with a Spartan courage and steel-nerved discipline worthy of the bravest of our fighting men.

... Spartan courage
and steel-nerved
discipline ...

*Document file Pegler D. H. Captain, 82/7/1 in the
Documents Department of the Imperial War Museum.*

## Sister Mary Fitzgibbon

*Of Queen Alexandra's Imperial Military Nursing Service, discovered that disease was as terrible a scourge at Gallipoli as battlefield injury.*

# . . . all suffering from dysentery and enteric.

We never got off the ship at all. They brought the boys down on stretchers or on muleback, down those steep paths on the cliffs that were almost vertical. We could see them from where we were. We spent weeks ploughing up and down the Dardanelles on the Essequibo… [a] Royal Mail ship. Small as it was, we couldn't go in near the shore because there were no harbours, no landing places. They brought the boys out on barges and laid them in stretchers that were really just shallow wooden boxes, two at a time, and then they were swung on to our ship by a crane. Most of the time we were under fire. The wounded were easy enough to deal with, but the sick! They were in a terrible state, all suffering from dysentery and enteric. Their insides had simply turned to water…

*From* The Roses of No Man's Land, *Lyn Macdonald, Penguin Books, 1993.*

## Lorna Neill

*Nineteen-year-old Lorna tells her mother how she has been helping French poilus in France. Too young to serve in any official capacity overseas, Lorna worked in a 'Cantine Anglaise' at Revigny in the Verdun sector, made possible by the generous donation of the steel magnate father of her friend and fellow worker, Maud Summers.*

The following is a list of things we gave out during February [1917], which is a short month.

250,000  cups of coffee
  15,000  cups of tea
  15,000  cups of chocolate
  22,000  cups of soup
302,000  total number of cups

Which as you will see makes an average of over 10,000 cups every twenty-four hours. In addition to that we gave 63,000 cigarettes, 3,500 presents, 600 loaves, 310 tins of beef.

That's not bad, is it?
Whew!

*From* The Roses of No Man's Land, *Lyn Macdonald, Penguin Books, 1993.*

## Mary Brough-Robertson, munitions worker

*Describes the lowly life of the munitions worker during World War I.*

Munitions workers were just about the lowest form of life in the eyes of the general public. We were supposed to make a great deal of money, and as other people didn't make so much they called us all sorts of things…

I can't speak of what people made making shells, but I know the wage for filling them was only twenty-five shillings [£1.25p] a week for a girl, which was no great sum. In fact, you couldn't manage with that amount, as you had to pay for all your meals, you didn't get any free. But when they finally went on strike the money was raised by 5s 6d (27½p) a week and they introduced a bonus system. You filled so many shells, and after that you got a bonus for how many shells you filled. This was a bad thing because it led to carelessness. The shells would come back to you as either too heavy or too light, and that was a bad thing because they might fall short when they were fired.

… you had to pay for all your meals, you didn't get any free.

*From a tape recording in the Imperial War Museum, quoted in* Forgotten Voices of the Great War, *Max Arthur, Ebury Press, 2002.*

## Bert Smith

*Bert Smith was eight years old when he witnessed the result of the Chilwell munitions factory explosion in Nottingham on 1 July 1918.*

I was having a game of cricket with my friends after school in the local recreation ground… and there was this almighty bang I felt at the back of my neck. It seemed to push me forward. I turned round to look and there was this huge cloud, a black cloud of smoke from ground level right to the heavens above. It seemed to be rolling and everybody on the recreation ground was looking at it with their mouths open. There were two old boys sitting under a tree and one said, 'That's Chilwell gone up'…

We got as far as Beeston and we couldn't get no farther on account of the people milling around the streets. So I sat down on the edge of the pavement and I could see a wagon coming. It must have been from the factory, and when it got level with me, only two feet away, there was a smell of burning rag. I looked and this wagon was piled up with bodies, stacked with bodies, must have been twenty or more, lashed on with ropes. There were half-naked, blackened bodies and the arms and legs were hanging over the side. I noticed there was blood trickling out the back of the wagon.

*Quoted in* All Quiet on the Home Front, *Richard Van Emden and Steve Humphries, Headline Book Publishing, 2004.*

## Brigadier General John Charteris

*The Brigadier noted this encounter in August 1916 in his diary.*

Yesterday I was motoring up towards Divisional Headquarters, when I overtook two young women on foot going the same way. I asked them what their destination was, and they said they wanted to walk to a unit in the front line to see what it was like to be under fire. I put them in a car going the other way and told them not to be naughty. They were both nurses at one of the casualty clearing stations having their day off. One of them was under twenty and said she was at school in August, 1914.

> I put them in a car going the other way and told them not to be naughty.

*From Charteris' book* At GHQ, *published Cassell, 1931, and quoted in* Call-To-Arms: The British Army 1914-1918, *Charles Messenger, Cassell Military Paperbacks, 2006.*

## Kitty Eckersley

*Kitty's husband Percy was killed in 1916, when she was several months pregnant with their child.*

It was a Monday morning [in 1915] and I was almost ready to go [to work at Noblet's Leather works at Ardenshaw] … there was a loud knocking on the door and this voice shouted 'Open the door – the Jerries are here!'… and in he came all mucky and what have you, straight from France.

But he was very dirty – filthy in fact. Even lousy. And mother said, 'You're not sleeping in one of my beds like that. There's a tub in the back,' she says, 'and you'd better get your things off.

Get them shirts and khaki off and whatnot and I'll see what I can do with it.' Eventually we found some old clothes of his that he had worn before, and he had a good rest.

All that day he was tired – he only got six days leave and he'd spent two of them travelling. . . I didn't go with him to the tram but one of my brothers did, with a friend of his. And it seems he told his friend, 'I'm afraid I shall never come back again.'

## 'Open the door – the Jerries are here!'

*From a tape recording in the Imperial War Museum, quoted in* Forgotten Voices of the Great War, *Max Arthur, Ebury Press, 2002.*

## Private Harold Carter

*Describes how shocked his mother was at his condition after arriving home on leave.*

I came home on leave from Ypres for four days. I got home, knocked at the door, and as they opened it I walked in and Mother rushed up as soon as she heard my voice. She was so pleased to see me she threw her arms round my neck and kissed me. Then she said, 'What's all this crawling about all over you?' I said, 'Well, mother, they're lice. Don't worry,' I said, but she was horrified. Of course, she never dreamed that conditions were such out there. I told her I'd have a wash down and dig out my civvy suit. Later on they asked me questions about what it was like over the other side but I didn't tell them too much. I didn't like to pile the agony on them at home. They knew that I'd had a rough time by looking at me – they didn't want telling twice.

> 'What's all this crawling about all over you?' I said, 'Well, mother, they're lice.'

*From a tape recording in the Imperial War Museum, quoted in* Forgotten Voices of the Great War, *Max Arthur, Ebury Press, 2002.*

## Vera Brittain, writer and pacifist

*A letter from Vera to her fiancé Roland Leighton, serving somewhere on the Western Front.*

**First London General Hospital**
**20 October 1915**

...The men being quite well apart from their wounds really makes it all the worse because they are so very conscious of the agony of having the wound dressed. I don't mind the general butcher's shop appearance, or holes in various parts of people that you could put your fist into, half so much as having to hold a head or leg for the Sister to dress it while the man moans & tries to squirm about. The orderlies won't do one or two of the dressings I have to help with — or rather, the Sisters won't have them, because they seem to be made sick so easily, & one of them who was holding a basin the other night fainted right on top of the patient.

> I don't mind the general butcher's shop appearance ...

*In* Letters From a Lost Generation, *edited by Alan Bishop and Mark Bostridge, p/b edition, Virago Press, 2008.*

## Private Dolly Shepherd, Women's Emergency Corps

*Describes her experience on volunteering for the Women's Emergency Corps.*

Directly the war started, I joined the Women's Emergency Corps. I went part-time up to this school in Baker Street [London]. I could only go in the evenings, but we had to give whatever time we could. I was a private, while people who could give all their time became officers. We had to supply our own uniforms – we bought everything.

It must have been with the permission of the War Office or someone, because a Grenadier Guardsman came to give us drill. Form fours, you know, real square-bashing. And he would say, 'And, about turn, about.' And he'd wait for a minute or two – and of course us in hobble skirts! And after he said, 'Turn!' he'd say, 'Do you know what you look like? A lot of jelly bags.'

> Directly the war started, I joined the Women's Emergency Corps.

*From a tape recording in the Imperial War Museum, quoted in* Forgotten Voices of the Great War, *Max Arthur, Ebury Press, 2002.*

## Sister Jentie Paterson

*Typed her first long letter for weeks, intending that it should be copied and sent to her family and friends in Scotland. Her father having sent an earlier letter to the local newspaper, whose editor published a 'wisely edited' version of it, Sister Paterson included him on her list of recipients.*

*No. 5 Clearing Station*
*Expeditionary Force,*
*G.P.O. London*

16 Nov. 1914

My dear Martha,

I received your p.c. of 20th-10-14 away up here today; it went to Versailles forwarded to Boulogne & then on here. I hear you say where is here? Well, we see the flashes of the guns & hear the roar day and night. We are the furthest up lot of sisters except those on the trains which have penetrated to within a mile or two of the lines. Last week one such train was under fire while they were moving in the wounded & they are the 1st sisters to be specially commended, we are dying for our turn next. This is the 1st time that these hospitals have ever had sisters attached & the added responsibility for the Colonel, as the Germans are treating us women so abominably, was not readily accepted. He told us frankly when we arrived he was greatly against us coming for reason stated & also because we would have to rough it & after this travel by motor, now he says he does not know what he would do without us . . .

*Document file Sister J. Paterson 90/10/1 in the Documents Department of the Imperial War Museum.*

## Mrs M. Hall, munitions worker

*Describes what it was like to work in a factory as a munitions worker.*

I'd never been in a factory before, but… I thought well, my brothers and my friends are in France, so a friend and I thought… let's do something. So we wrote to London and asked for war work. And we were directed to a munitions factory at Perivale in London. We had to have a health examination because we had to be very physically fit – perfect eyesight and strong. We had to supply four references, and be British-born of British parents …

It was a perfect factory to work in: everybody seemed unaware of the powder around them, unaware of any danger.… There wasn't any big explosion during the three years I was there. We worked at making these little pellets, very innocent-looking little pellets, but had there been the slightest grit in those pellets, it would have been 'Goodbye'.

After each day when we got home we had a lovely good wash. And believe me the water was blood-red and our skin was perfectly yellow, right down through the body, legs and toenails even, perfectly yellow. In some people it caused a very nasty rash all round the chin. It was a shame because we were a bevy of beauties, you know…

In some people it caused a very nasty rash …

*From a tape recording in the Imperial War Museum, quoted in* Forgotten Voices of the Great War, *Max Arthur, Ebury Press, 2002.*

# OVER THERE

# Over There

When war broke out in Europe in August 1914, the view of most Americans was that it was none of their business. If the Europeans wanted to break each other's heads, let them get on with it. For their part, none of the European combatants considered America at all when it came to working out war strategies and plans of action: the American army was insignificantly small, ill-trained, had little equipment, and was on the other side of the Atlantic.

Although the United States declared its neutrality in the European war, this did not stop American citizens going to Europe in sizeable numbers to help, either in a voluntary capacity, or by offering their services to the British and French armies, this despite the fact that American law did not permit any American to join a foreign army and retain his US citizenship. (This law was quietly waived in 1917, when America did enter the war, thus allowing US citizens to transfer to their own country's forces.)

When the United States declared its neutrality in 1914, it expected that its shipping would be allowed to pass freely across the Atlantic. This was fine while the Royal Navy controlled the sea-lanes, but as more and more German submarines began operating in the Atlantic, the position was hard to maintain.

As early as May 1915, America was

alerted to the ability of Germany to put American lives in danger on the high seas. On 7 May, the Cunard liner, the *Lusitania* was sunk by a torpedo from a German submarine. The liner had left New York on May Day, carrying 1,256 passengers, among them many Americans, including the multimillionaire sportsman, Alfred G. Vanderbilt. She sank in twelve minutes, drowning 1,198 of her passengers, of whom 128, including Mr Vanderbilt, were American. Almost at once, the American Red Cross, which had been doing good work on both sides of the front line, withdrew its workers from the German side.

The United States severed relations with Germany on 3 February 1917 and Congress declared war on 6 April. By this time, the Allies in Europe, France's General Foch in particular, were realising that if they hoped to beat the Germans on the battlefield they would need the armed forces of the United States of America to help them do it. By the end of May, when Congress enacted the draft, it was clear that they would get them.

Since the second largest white, European ethnic group in America was German, from the American government's point of view it clearly became necessary for Americans to be persuaded, not only to think that getting involved in the war in Europe was a patriotic thing to do, but also to learn to dislike Germans and treat them with suspicion. Taking a lead from the British and French, the American Government began a major anti-German propaganda campaign, organised through a Committee of Public Information. Soon, Americans were being fed the same sort of propaganda – the dismemberment of children and the rape of women by German soldiers, the deliberate destruction and fouling of churches, etc, etc – that sections of the British popular press had been putting out since 1914.

This sort of propaganda was repeated in the training of the thousands of young men now drafted into the US fighting forces. Many American 'Doughboys' – a nickname arising from the fact that the big, round, brass buttons on the uniforms of the Federal Troops in the Civil War looked like 'doughboys', or dumplings – thought like Private Joseph Sisenwein, 307th Infantry, who talked about 'our Great Adventure. We didn't know where we were going and we didn't give a whoop.' They were also very happy to be going 'over there', to 'save the world's women and children from the Kaiser's murderous armies'. There was good reason for George M. Cohan to give the title 'Over There' to one of America's most famous songs of the Great War.

The American Expeditionary Force (AEF), commanded by General John J. Pershing, began moving over the Atlantic to France in June 1917. The American troops' general cheerfulness and optimism, their singing as they hiked through much of France and eventually dug themselves in on the front line astonished the war-weary and exhausted Europeans.

The first American offensive of any size in the Great War was at Cantigny at the end of May 1918. By early August 1918 the AEF was beginning to play a big part in the Allies' advance to victory, in battles along the Western Front from the Channel to Verdun and beyond. In September, when the battles of the St. Mihiel salient became the American forces' first big offensive, the First American Army consisted of twenty combat divisions. Other AEF divisions were fighting with the British and French armies.

During September and October 1918, the Meuse-Argonne offensive really began the business of turning the American Army into one of the world's leading military powers. In this mighty offensive, the American First Army, which General Pershing had built up in the late summer, took more than a million troops into battle, supported by 2,500 heavy guns, 800 aircraft and 300 tanks. It was the greatest battle fought by American troops who, in the forty-seven days it lasted, fired more ammunition than was used in the whole of the American Civil War. Casualties were high: 26,000 men killed, and almost 97,000 wounded. American military might stepped on to the world stage in 1918.

## John Laffin, military historian

*Wrote several eyewitness accounts of the scene in Paris when the first Doughboys marched into town, in his book,* Americans in Battle.

The arrival of the first battalion of Americans in Paris was an even more extraordinary occasion. On the march to La Fayette's tomb the battalion was joined by a great crowd, many women forcing their way into the ranks and swinging along arm-in-arm with the Doughboys. With wreaths about their necks and bouquets in their hats and on their rifles the column looked, according to Pershing, like a 'moving flower garden'. Without formation the animated throng pushed its way through avenues of people to the martial strains of a French band and the din of cheers. Many French people dropped to their knees as the Doughboys went by.

## . . . many women forcing their way into the ranks and swinging along arm-in-arm with the Doughboys.

*From* Americans in Battle, *John Laffin, J.M. Dent and Sons, London, 1973.*

## General Foch

*The French commander commenting on the first American troops to arrive in France. General Foch was much inclined to be admiring, so concerned was he to get the help of American troops in the war.*

We were impressed by the height of the men, by their well-fitting uniforms, by their physical development and poise, by their splendid health and vigour. If their gait lacked something of suppleness, this defect was compensated by the accuracy and precision of movement altogether remarkable.

## A French reporter

*Working for the publication L'Illustration: a very unfair crack at his own country's troops who had endured three years of brutal fighting and had become much hardened in the process.*

One of these first Americans, arriving at St Nazaire, shouted from the gangplank, 'I have come to fight all the kings!'... These young men with their lithe and muscled bodies, their smooth faces and springy steps, resembled players on the gridiron but did not in the least evoke our heavy, unkempt and untidy poilus.

... this defect was compensated by the accuracy and precision of movement altogether remarkable.

## The American Infantry Pack

The American soldier's pack is the result of an exhaustive study of the subject made by a board of officers of the Army. It was adopted by the Government in 1910. It is essentially an American institution, original in design and construction. It is based upon ideas of how the American Indian squaw carries her papoose and how the American woodsman carries his load.

It is the lightest as well as the most scientifically constructed Infantry pack in the world.

It is based upon ideas of how the American Indian squaw carries her papoose . . .

The Infantry Soldier's Handbook, *by Major William H. Waldron, U.S. Infantry, published in 1917. (Taken from an edition published by The Lyons Press, 2006.)*

## Major Garretson

*Celebrating the Fourth of July, 1918, in France.*

On the Fourth of July the whole of France and England made a gala day of it, and it was indeed a curious privilege to be in a British Army Service School and hear British Officers toasting the United States for the courage it showed a hundred and fifty years ago in insisting on personal liberty, and fighting a mad German prince to get it. It may be said to the Briton's credit, there was never a word of regret about lost territory or anything of that sort, which was quite remarkable when you think of the Briton's love for empire beyond the sea.

*Getting at least one fairly quiet day during the American action in the Meuse-Argonne offensive.*

Friday morning [in late September 1918] the engineers managed to straighten out a couple of dugouts, which gave us some shelter, and by Friday noon the General's cook had put together some coffee and bacon which helped. Friday noon along came the Division Adjutant and handed me my Majority, and Friday afternoon I also got in a shave and brushed my teeth. Friday night I managed to get five hours sleep in a fairly dry place, so by Saturday morning was moderately respectable.

*Document file Major L. B. Garretson, 95/6/1 in the Documents Department of the Imperial War Museum.*

## Sinking of the *Lusitania*

*New Yorkers read of the sinking of the* Lusitania *in* The World *newspaper, which also told its readers that President Wilson was 'stunned' and that this was the tensest situation in America since the Spanish-American War.*

London, May 8 – The Cunard liner *Lusitania* was torpedoed, supposedly by German submarines, shortly after 2 o'clock yesterday afternoon, ten miles off the Old Head of Kinsale, on the south coast of Munster, Ireland.

She sank fifteen minutes later. The company states that no warning was given her. Passengers and crew, the *Lusitania* carried 2,104 persons when she sailed from New York, on May 1. The meagre, confused reports so far received make it uncertain how many of them have been saved.

A steward of the first boat that reached Queenstown – forty miles by sea from Kinsale – with survivors from the liner, said he feared that 900 lives had been lost.

This dispatch came from Queenstown at 1.10 a.m.:

*The tug* Stormcock *has returned here, bringing about 150 survivors of the* Lusitania, *principally passengers, among whom were many women, several of the crew and one steward. Describing the experience of the* Lusitania, *the steward said:*

'The passengers were at lunch when a submarine came up and fired two torpedoes, which struck the *Lusitania* on the starboard side, one forward and one in the engine room. They caused terrific explosions. Capt. Turner immediately ordered the boats out. The ship began to list badly immediately.

'Ten boats were put into the water, and between 400 and 500 passengers entered them. The boat in which I was approached the land with three other boats, and we were picked up shortly after 4 o'clock by the *Stormcock*. I fear that few of the officers were saved. They acted bravely.

'There was only fifteen minutes from the time the ship was struck until she foundered, going down bow foremost. It was a dreadful sight.'

'There was only fifteen minutes from the time the ship was struck until she foundered, going down bow foremost. It was a dreadful sight.'

## Corporal Sam M. Ross, 165th Infantry Regiment (69th New York)

*Discovers there's no likelihood of singing on a French troop train.*

**8 April 1918**

At 2 p.m. we started – We had a four hour hike and had to carry more than on any other hike. We had to carry all we owned except two blankets, it was the hardest short hike yet. We reached the R R station about 6.30. Our 'Pullmans' were waiting for us. As they had been used by cows previously we had to clean them out. Then we had mess. About 8 p.m. we piled in, 30 in a car; after about thirty minutes whistling and half a dozen attempts, we got started – our engine was about as big as a Ford.

Thirty men with packs in one of these cars can't all sit on the floor. You sit down in layers and if you happen to be in the bottom layer, you can't move without disturbing the other 29 and the other 29 won't be disturbed, so you don't move. It is worse than six in a 7 x 7 wall tent. We had with us several singers, but the little train was so noisy it was no use, so we waited and hoped there would be a wreck or something and once in a while you would fall half asleep. As soon as you did, the engineer would blow the whistle. If you ever heard a French train whistle, you would know why the sound of a cannon is music to the Froggies.

## . . . the little train was so noisy it was no use . . .

*Document file S. M. Ross 81/14/1, in the Documents Department of the Imperial War Museum.*

# ARMISTICE AND AFTER

# Armistice and After

At ten minutes past five in the morning on 11 November 1918 representatives of Germany signed the terms for an armistice, which would come into force at 11 a.m. that same day. At 7.35 a.m. the British Fourth Army sent a message, similar to ones being sent to commanders throughout the Western Front, in Italy, in Greece, in Turkey and the Middle East, saying 'Hostilities will cease at 1100 hours today November 11. Troops will stand fast on line reached at that hour which will be reported by wire to adv. Army Hdqrs. as soon as possible. Defensive precautions will be maintained. There will be no intercourse of any description with the enemy until receipt of instructions from Army Headquarters.'

Thus the most destructive war the world had seen – the 'war to end all wars' – came to an end. Queen Mary wrote in her diary that this was 'the greatest day in world history'. Most of the men and women involved in the war were probably too exhausted to agree with her.

In the near six hours between the signing of the Armistice and its coming into effect, many hundreds more soldiers on both sides died, many of them killed by small arms fire, since the big guns ceased firing before 11 o'clock, but others killed because their officers decided to carry on the fight until the bitter end, or, on the Allied side, because they thought that they could move with impunity into

German-held areas before 11 a.m. Some ten million soldiers, the great majority of them young men – a 'lost generation', as they were called – did not return home. The fighting men knew, when they signed on, that should they be killed in action, their bodies would be buried on the field of battle.

Two Britons were brought home and buried in state after the war. One was the 'Unknown Warrior' who was interred with full military honours in Westminster Abbey on 11 November 1920. The other was Nurse Edith Cavell, who had been shot by the Germans in 1915 for helping British prisoners-of-war to escape. Her body was brought back to England in May 1919 and her funeral cortège was watched by very large crowds as it made its way through London for a service in Westminster Abbey.

Of the British servicemen who did return, 80,000 were disabled and many more suffered for months and years from shell shock. They did not come back to 'a land fit for heroes' as the politicians had hoped. Even though the women who had been doing their jobs during the war were sent back home to make way for them, there were not enough jobs to go round and soon unemployment stalked the land. With it, for many in the poorer classes, also came hunger.

Food shortage had become a major problem for many in the last years of the war, as the German submarine fleet in the Atlantic gained a stranglehold on shipping. Hunger remained a problem for many well into the 1920s. At the huge Hunger March along Whitehall in 1920, thousands of the marchers, as well as many of the police who opposed them, wore campaign medals and ribbons on their chests.

Another horror that did not end with the Armistice was the influenza epidemic that killed many Britons in the final year of the war. The 'Spanish lady', as the flu was called, struck in mid-1918 and killed probably more than 200,000 people before it finally abated in the spring of 1919.

In the long term – the very long term, it seemed to some – improved health for everyone was one of the positive outcomes of the Great War. The government and medical people had been so shocked by the poor state of health of many thousands of the men who had volunteered or attested to serve – four out of five of the thousands of men considered unfit for military service had poor, or no teeth, and many others had grown up so undernourished that they did not reach the very low height standard. After the war, the first steps were taken along the road to introducing a national health service in Britain.

## Webster

*An old soldier named Webster foreseeing the end of the war in 1917, for the benefit of 16-year-old Private Thomas Hope.*

I'll tell you what will happen to you duration soldiers [when the war is over]. You'll have the time of your lives, you'll be hugged and kissed, treated and petted, they'll have banners strung across the streets: 'Welcome Home, Our Heroic Tommies'... you'll be the heaven and earth and all that therein is for just one month, then some morning they'll wake up and realise the war is over, and that's when you fellows will have to start using your own toilet paper. You'll get the cold shoulder, as they'll have no more use for a penniless, out-of-work, fighting man who stinks of trench manners and speech...

> You'll get the cold shoulder, as they'll have no more use for a penniless, out-of-work, fighting man . . .

*Quoted in* Boy Soldiers of the Great War, *Richard van Emden, Headline Book Publishing, 2005.*

## General Erich Ludendorff

*Germany's military leader recollecting the last months of the Great War.*

I was told of behaviour which, I openly confess, I should not have thought possible in the German army; whole bodies of our men had surrendered to single troopers, or isolated squadrons. Retiring troops, meeting a fresh division going bravely into action, had shouted out things like 'Blackleg', and 'You're prolonging the war.'

'At eleven o'clock this morning the war will be over.'

## Diplomat Harold Nicolson

*Describes witnessing an historic Armistice Day moment from his window in the Foreign Office. In 1919, Nicolson was one of the British diplomats who attended the great Peace Conference in Paris that resulted in the Treaty of Versailles.*

It was 10.55 am. Suddenly the front door [of No. 10 Downing Street] opened. Mr Lloyd George, his white hair fluttering on the wind, appeared on the front doorstep. He waved his arms outwards. I opened the window hurriedly. He was shouting the same sentence over and over again. I caught his words. 'At eleven o'clock this morning the war will be over.'

## Robert Graves, author

# I was still mentally and nervously organized for war.

At the Peace Day celebrations in the castle [Harlech], I was asked, as the senior Man of Harlech who had served overseas, to make a speech about the glorious dead. I spoke in commendation of the Welshman as a fighting man and earned loud cheers. But not only did I have no experience of independent civilian life, having gone straight from school into the army: I was still mentally and nervously organized for war. Shells used to come bursting on my bed at midnight, even though Nancy [his wife] shared it with me; strangers in daytime would assume the faces of friends who had been killed. When strong enough to climb the hill behind Harlech and revisit my favourite country, I could not help seeing it as a prospective battlefield. I would find myself working out tactical problems, planning how best to hold the Upper Artro valley against an attack from the sea, or where to place a Lewis gun if I were trying to rush Dolwreiddiog Farm from the brow of the hill, and what would be the best cover for my rifle-grenade section.

*From* Goodbye to All That, *first published by Jonathan Cape, 1929, rev. ed. 1957. Robert Graves died in 1985.*

## Martin Marix Evans, military historian

*Tells of one death among many in the last hours of the Great War.*

On 10 November, at about 2300 hours, the Canadians had begun their quiet entry into Mons. The 5th Lancers, who had fought here in the famous battle of 1914, took St Denis.... One of the 2nd Division's battalions, the 28th North West, went beyond Havre to Ville-sur-Haine. There, at 10.58 hours, a Canadian soldier was talking to excited villagers outside 71 rue de Mons when a shot rang out. Private George L. Price fell dead.

. . . a shot rang out. Private George L. Price fell dead.

*From* 1918: The Year of Victories, *by Martin Marix Evans, Arcturus in assn. with W. Foulsham & Co., 2002.*

## Lieutenant Godfrey Buxton

*6th Battalion, Duke of Wellington's Regiment.*

We didn't have dentists in any great number until 1916. Then when the dentists came over and the men got their teeth put right, and the dead ones pulled out and so on, it certainly got them into another era of health, because then their food could be properly digested. It seems a small thing, but it was of tremendous value when these dentists came and improved teeth.

Until then I don't think the public were as conscious of the value of teeth. And I believe it began a tremendous change in the attitude of the working classes after the war – quite new to what had happened before it.

> We didn't have dentists in any great number until 1916.

*From a tape recording in the Imperial War Museum, quoted in* Forgotten Voices of the Great War, *Max Arthur, Ebury Press in association with the Imperial War Museum, 2002.*

## Major Leland B. Garretson

*Commanding the 315th Machine Gun Battalion, 80th Division, U.S. Army sums up his thoughts on the horrors of war a day after the Armistice.*

12 November 1918
It is a perfectly glorious day and peace at last reigns over this weary war scarred land. We are out in the country, in fact our camp is on part of the old Battle Field and Boche wire put there in 1914 still runs within fifty yards of my P.C. Although all of us are of course ready to toss our hats in the air and howl with joy under it all I believe most of us find ourselves thanking God over and over again that this terrible thing is really and truly over. It is hard to realise that the harvest of all our efforts over the past year and a half is actually at hand, and that our aims are nearly accomplished. While of course we still have no end of work to do, the fact remains that the pent up horrors of Imperialism are forever dead, and I thank God for one that I was allowed to do my very humble part in bringing it about. We all realise that our Division is not an old campaigning Division when compared to the French and British veterans, but during the short time we were at it, we were made to pay our precious toll and came to the thorough realisation that modern war is the most wholly awful thing ever conceived by the mind of man, and that the Boche besides being a very worthy foe is the arch master of it all.

*Document file Major L. B. Garretson, 95/6/1 in the Documents Department of the Imperial War Museum.*

## Major Keith, Officer in the Australian Corps

# 'I wonder what we are all going to do next?'

At 11 o'clock on 11 November I was sitting in a room in the Brewer's House at Le Cateau which had been Sir John French's headquarters at the time of the battle of Mons. I was… with a major in the Scots Greys who had a large, old-fashioned hunting watch which he put on the table and watched the minutes go round. When 11 o'clock came, he shut his watch up and said, 'I wonder what we are all going to do next?' That was very much the feeling of everyone…

Nearby there was a German machine-gun unit giving our troops a lot of trouble. They kept on firing until practically 11 o'clock. At precisely 11 o'clock an officer stepped out of their position, stood up, lifted his helmet and bowed to the British officers. He then fell in all his men in front of the trench and marched them off. I always thought that this was a wonderful display of confidence in British chivalry, because the temptation to fire on them must have been very great.

*From a tape recording in the Imperial War Museum, quoted in* Forgotten Voices of the Great War, *Max Arthur, Ebury Press in association with the Imperial War Museum, 2002.*

## Robert Graves

*Recounted in* Goodbye To All That *the sad story of his mother-in-law's death during the first wave of the Spanish influenza outbreak.*

Nancy's brother, Tony, had also gone to France now, and her mother made herself ill by worrying about him.... The first Spanish influenza epidemic began, and Nancy's mother caught it, but did not want to miss Tony's leave and going to the London theatres with him. So when the doctor came, she took quantities of aspirin, reduced her temperature, and pretended to be all right.... She died in London on July 13th, a few days later. Her chief solace, as she lay dying, was that Tony got his leave prolonged on her account.

> Nancy's mother caught it, but did not want to miss Tony's leave ...

*From* All Quiet on the Home Front, *Richard van Emden and Steve Humphries, Headline Book Publishing, 2004.*

## Gunner L. G. Whiteley

*Thus ended Gunner Whiteley's war, which he served in the Royal Field Artillery, and which had begun more than four years before, when his brother had 'volunteered' him in September 1914 and he had rejoined his Territorial Army unit.*

January 15, 1919. At last I had my Medical Board [at a dispersal hospital, the Keighley War Hospital] and had to be examined by two army doctors and one civilian.

The elderly Colonel in charge of the Board looked over my notes and said, 'Well, laddie, you are fine. I have scrutinised your medical history. You have been wounded in the thigh, had extensive Mustard Gas burns, Trench foot, septicaemia – and you are in excellent condition. I only wish my heart and lungs were in as good a state as yours. We shall grade you A1. Good luck to you.'

January 16. I collected my discharge papers, a civilian ration book and a leave pass to cover the next 28 days. I got a bus to the station, a train to Halifax and, having all the time in the world at my disposal, I took the tram to Sowerby Bridge. Riding on the top deck, I took in all the old views…

February 10. Today my leave pass expired, my army pay ceased & I resumed work in the drawing office of Pollitt and Wigzell's Mill and Foundry.

*Document file L. G. Whiteley, 06/55/1 in the Documents Department of the Imperial War Museum.*

## Corporal Clifford Lane
*1st Battalion, Hertfordshire Regiment.*

As far as the Armistice itself was concerned, it was a kind of anticlimax. We were too far gone, too exhausted, really, to enjoy it. All we wanted to do was go back to our billets, there was no cheering, no singing. That day we had no alcohol at all. We simply celebrated the Armistice in silence and thankfulness that it was all over. And I believe that happened quite a lot in France. It was such a sense of anticlimax. We were drained of all emotion. That's what it amounted to.

> . . . it was a kind of anticlimax. We were too far gone, too exhausted, to enjoy it.

*From a tape recording in the Imperial War Museum, quoted in* Forgotten Voices of the Great War, *Max Arthur, Ebury Press in association with the Imperial War Museum, 2002.*

## Alice Mckinnon

*Returned home from two years' nursing in France at the end of the war. By chance, she was in London on the day of Edith Cavell's service in Westminster Abbey.*

I was walking along the street with my suitcase when I heard that Edith Cavell's funeral procession was to pass through that part of town… So I decided to stay where I was on the spot and pay my respects. I put the suitcase down and sat on it and waited. The traffic was going past, you know how noisy traffic can be, when suddenly it all went quiet, very quiet. There wasn't a sound and then they came along, and I put my head down and I cried and cried. Somebody asked me afterwards did she have a horse-drawn hearse and I said I didn't really see; I was so upset.

> There wasn't a sound and then they came along, and I put my head down and I cried and cried.

*From* All Quiet on the Home Front, *Richard van Emden and Steve Humphries, Headline Book Publishing, 2004.*

## Siegfried Sassoon
*in London on 11 November 1918.*

[I] found masses of people in streets and congested Tubes, all waving flags and making fools of themselves – an outburst of mob patriotism. It was a wretched wet night, and very mild. It is a loathsome ending to the loathsome tragedy of the last four years.